the family kitchen

the family kitchen

easy and delicious recipes
for parents and kids
to make and enjoy together

Debra Ponzek

Clarkson Potter/Publishers
New York

Copyright © 2006 by Debra Ponzek
Photographs © 2006 by Alexandra Grablewski

Published in the United States by Clarkson Potter/Publishers, an imprint of
the Crown Publishing Group, a division of Random House, Inc., New York.
www.crownpublishing.com
www.clarksonpotter.com

Clarkson N. Potter is a trademark and Potter and colophon are registered
trademarks of Random House, Inc.

Library of Congress Cataloging-in-Publication Data
    Ponzek, Debra.
    The family kitchen: easy and delicious recipes for parents and kids
to make and enjoy together / by Debra Ponzek.—1st ed.
    I. Cookery.   I. Title.
TX652.5P66   2006
641.5—dc22   2005017649

ISBN-13: 978-1-4000-8280-3
ISBN-10: 1-4000-8280-3

Printed in China

Design by Maggie Hinders

10   9   8   7   6   5   4   3   2   1

First Edition

To my children, Remy, Cole, and Gray. I'm so happy to share the
kitchen with your smiling faces and I look forward to more
years of fun-filled cooking adventures!
Love, Mom

acknowledgments

Thanks to:

Mary Goodbody, whose exceptional writing made our collaboration effortless. She captured my voice and helped me say exactly what I wanted to say, just how I wanted to say it.

My agent, Jane Dystel, who is always in my corner and whose belief in this book was steadfast from the very beginning.

Pam Krauss at Clarkson Potter, whose clear vision helped me focus and produce the book I truly wanted.

Rica Allannic and Aliza Fogelson: a big thanks to these great editors and especially to Rica, whose eagle eye helped polish the manuscript. Thanks, Rica, for your painstaking care.

Maggie Hinders, whose stunning design makes this book so beautiful.

Marysarah Quinn, Mark McCauslin, and Felix Gregorio, who made sure the production process went smoothly and we stayed on schedule.

Alexandra Grablewski, whose beautiful photographs make the food look so good and whose easygoing, friendly nature made the photo shoot days relaxed and fun.

Bonnie Suarez, who, when I needed extra help, tested and retested many of the recipes.

Justin Sullivan and the staff at Aux Délices, who kept me so well organized while I was writing this book that the business ran like clockwork.

Finally, to Greg, the most supportive and wonderful husband in the world. Thank you for trying all my kitchen experiments!

contents

introduction

So much has happened since I left my job as chef of Montrachet, the acclaimed New York City restaurant, to move to Connecticut about ten years ago, it's hard to know where to begin. I haven't stopped working. In fact, my three specialty food stores, all called Aux Délices, keep me busier than ever, but the real change in my life can be summed up in one word: kids.

Surely I am not the only mother who can barely recall what it was like before three kids took over the house, the car, the backyard, and my heart, and it's precisely because of this 180-degree turnaround that I wanted to write this book. The book is for moms and dads who like to cook, who want to teach their kids proficiency in the kitchen, and who want to eat well—without pretension—when they find time to cook at home. Above all, this book is about the possibilities for connecting with your kids and enjoying your family by cooking together.

I cook dinner nearly every night of the week. Sure, we go out occasionally (I love to try new restaurants whenever I can) and buy takeout now and then, but overall, my husband, Greg, and I believe meals are important and something to anticipate happily every day. Quite frankly, I have an easier time getting through a long or even disastrous day knowing that in the end, I'll sit down, surrounded by my family, for dinner. The trouble is, too often, time at the table is short. Someone has homework, a meeting, or a bath and suddenly, dinner is over.

Long ago, I decided to bring the kids into the kitchen with me to teach them cooking fundamentals. I soon realized that an added benefit was the time I got to spend with one, two, or all three of my children as we measured, stirred, tasted, and seasoned. It pretty much extended the dinner hour. It's easy to talk and laugh when everyone is focused on a task. The kitchen is warm, the pace is relaxed, and the conversation invariably runs deeper than, "How was school?" "Fine."

Kids are so proud when they create something in the kitchen for everyone to eat. I recall how excited I was when I first discovered I could make dinner for my family and that they *liked* it! Your kids will enjoy a sense of accomplishment when they cook, and yet there's nothing competitive about it. Even the flops can taste good!

I love cooking with my kids and they learn more and more every day, from math skills and something about nutrition to geography and history. Cooking together opens the door to discussions about the environment, where food comes from, and how it travels from place to place. And when, years from now, they go out into the world, I will be confident that they are well armed with one of life's essential tools: knowing how to cook. With luck, they will recall all the good food we ate and all the fun we had along the way and will want to share a similar experience with their own children.

A lot of kids grow up today without rudimentary culinary skills, which I believe are valuable life skills, and it's up to us as parents to teach them. If you yourself like to cook, that's half the battle! On the other hand, food and cooking have taken center stage in much of America's collective consciousness, and children who might watch the Food Network or read about chefs in magazines want to be part of the scene.

I don't care if my kids grow up to be chefs. I do care that they appreciate good food, know where it comes from, can find their way around a kitchen, and know how to eat healthfully. While I haven't read scientific studies about it, it is my experience that kids are more apt to try a new food if they have helped prepare a dish. I encourage my kids to smell, touch, even nibble on unfamiliar ingredients. They might decide they don't like something once it's cooked, but if they experience the parts that make the whole, they are more likely to develop curiosity and may well try the food another time.

I didn't intend to be a chef, but after two years studying biomedical engineering at Boston University, I decided engineering wasn't for me. I turned to some friends who owned the Grove Street Café in Greenwich Village to talk about my interest in cooking, and they urged me to look into culinary schools. Until then, I had not considered studying cooking, but as soon as I began at the Culinary Institute of America, I loved it! I was very happy, too, during the following years when I worked in high-end restaurants in

New Jersey and Manhattan. The three-star reviews I earned three times from the *New York Times* while the chef at Montrachet were immensely rewarding, and the various chef awards and commendations were equally gratifying. After a while, though, I felt restless, eager to learn something new and own a business. Being a serious chef and someone who loved good food, gourmet takeout food appealed to me. I saw its potential in the marketplace and decided to take the plunge. In 1994, I walked out of the restaurant kitchen and moved to coastal Connecticut to open the first Aux Délices in Riverside, Connecticut, with my husband, Greg Addonizio. I opened the second in downtown Greenwich in 2000, and the third in Darien, Connecticut, in 2004. We also found time to have three kids!

Aux Délices is a food shop specializing in high-end takeout food with a decidedly Provençal accent for very American palates. (We also have a full-service catering business that we run out of Stamford, Connecticut.) At all three store locations, we serve breakfast, lunch, and dinner, which some of our customers choose to eat in the store and many more take home. Throughout the book, I make references to a number of our more popular or especially family-friendly dishes.

The recipes are all tried and true, whether they originated in the kitchens of Aux Délices or in my home kitchen. I selected only those that can be made with your kids at your side, helping in small or more significant ways. As a family, we cook some of them over and over and others only now and then, which is how most people cook. I know my kids like these dishes, as do Greg and I. You won't find recipes for pizzas with funny faces or endless pasta dishes in this book. Cookbooks directed at kids are great and can be a lot of fun, but my intent is to give families an intriguing variety of recipes that appeals to everyone's sensibilities and tastes and addresses how we cook and eat today. This is food you really will want to eat every day—there is nothing gimmicky here. The book is designed for casual meals where everyone, from kids to grandmothers to next-door neighbors, might find their way to your table.

I organized the book into meal courses—breakfast, lunch, dinner, and dessert—and added a few more chapters to appeal especially to parents and kids. I include a group of recipes that might be fun to prepare on a snow day, or others that you and the kids could make for a bake sale at school. I have ideas for a summertime backyard supper or a picnic in the park. These are not rigid menus but ideas to use as jumping-off points for family meals.

As my kids have grown, I have discovered what fun it is to cook with them, even after a long day at work. In the next chapter, I explain how you can organize your time and your kitchen and gauge your kids' abilities so that cooking with them is rewarding, not maddening. As you make a weekday dinner or bake a special cake together, you create food memories and share your time with those who will treasure them most. I don't expect my kids to thank me for all the recipes they learned along the way—or at least not until they have children of their own, perhaps—but I cherish the time we spend together. I wouldn't trade the spilled flour and sticky countertops for anything!

cooking with the kids

My kids range in age from nine to four, with my daughter, Remy, being the oldest, and my sons, Cole and Gray, following her. All three eagerly join me in the kitchen to prepare a meal. This isn't because of some weird cooking gene or because we don't allow them to watch TV until they beat the egg whites, but because I've always included them in this daily activity as part of our routine. Like any other life skill, learning how to cook happens over time. I started cooking as a child and even today, after cooking professionally for twenty years, I am still learning.

In this chapter, I list organizational, safety, and sanitation tips and pass on what I consider commonsense advice for families who cook together. I can't emphasize enough how important it is to rely on your own judgment; you know your children better than anyone else. This is why I never list specific tasks as being "age-appropriate." Your daughter may be ready to pull hot baking sheets from the oven at ten, while someone else's child would not be. Every parent knows to err on the side of caution around hot stoves and sharp food processor blades, and parents know best when to trust their kids to move on to the next level of responsibility.

CALL THE KIDS

I've arranged the recipes in every chapter in order of difficulty. The first few recipes will be easier than the last ones, but this does not necessarily mean they are quicker. I am far more interested in good technique and good flavor than in shortcuts.

With every recipe, I have a section labeled "Call the Kids" followed by bulleted ideas for tasks the kids can undertake for that particular dish. This is not a didactic list but instead is a guide to let you, the parent, know how much kids can do in each recipe. And regardless of what I list, you will have to rely on your judgment when it comes to your own children. Even a very young child can handle a whisk or rubber spatula.

To help, in some recipes I list certain tasks under a subheading called "Use Your Judgment." These always involve handling hot pans, using a food processor, and knife work. Teaching budding cooks to use knives imparts a valuable skill but can be dangerous. Some children are adept and responsible enough at ten or eleven to use a knife, while others might not be ready for a few more years. If you feel your kids can handle knives, I urge you to let them use knives that are properly sharpened; every cook knows that dull knives are more dangerous than those with sharp blades. If they are too young for sharp knives, let them use blunt knives or plastic knives for simple kitchen tasks such as cutting soft fruit or bread.

I hope a quick glance at the "Call the Kids" lists will lower stress levels. You'll see how well suited a particular recipe is for your kids. You'll see how much they can do and decide if calling them into the kitchen will be helpful—or not. (I admit that there are times when it's far easier to do it yourself!) You may decide, after reading one of these lists, that there is a chore your three-year-old could do, such as tearing up lettuce leaves or rinsing vegetables under running water. You may also see how more experienced teens could put an entire dish together while you tend to another.

KITCHEN SENSE

Not everyone has a large kitchen and even the most spacious can feel crowded with too many cooks. Consider following a system used in professional kitchens and assign your child a spot that is all his. This "station" is an area of the kitchen with a clear countertop where he works, where his tools are assembled, and where sisters and brothers cannot intrude. Make sure there's easy access to the sink, refrigerator, and garbage can.

The best way to help your kids learn organization is to read through a recipe before you begin. Discuss what bowls, measuring cups, pots, and pans are needed. Decide on spoons and whisks. Have the children gather the utensils and other equipment they need before they begin cooking. Next, help them find the ingredients for the tasks assigned to them. Arrange everything on the countertops. Pull up a stool, if needed, so that the child can easily reach the counter.

Cleaning up as you go along is smart but not always practical. If one child is rinsing green beans in a colander and her little brother tries to wash out a mixing bowl, pandemonium might be just around the corner. Children have small hands and don't have the dexterity we do and so there are bound to be spills. Be patient. Sure, the kitchen may look like a cyclone hit when the kids help you prepare dinner, but unless you are extremely tired or pressed for time, you won't care. The fun and the company are more than fair compensation.

SAFETY FIRST

Every professional kitchen I have worked in has safety rules. High flames, sharp knives, and slippery surfaces invite disaster! The same is true of home kitchens, which, while more benign than professional ones, still have more potential for accidents than any other room in the house.

Along with safety comes sanitation. Clean kitchens and good habits greatly reduce the risk of picking up bacteria, germs, or viruses.

Because of this, I am keenly aware of safety and sanitation and teach my kids the basics of both. No need to frighten anyone, but a few commonsense precautions make a big difference and when these are observed, everyone can relax and have a good time together.

- Don't let kids cook without adult supervision.
- Tie back long hair; remove dangling jewelry; tuck in loose clothing.
- Wash hands with warm soap and water before beginning any recipe. Wash them again if you leave the kitchen for any reason.
- Wash cutting boards after use, especially after cutting meat, poultry, or fish on them.
- Never let children use sharp knives without adult supervision. (And make sure all knives are properly sharpened.)
- Transfer knives by putting them on the countertop rather than handing them from person to person.
- Never put sharp knives in the sink where they might get covered by other kitchen equipment and so could stab an unsuspecting hand. Put them on the cutting board or wash them as you use them.

- Encourage kids to use blunt butter knives or plastic knives to cut soft fruit and vegetables.
- Pull up a stool or sturdy chair so that kids can reach the counter.
- Don't let kids use electrical appliances without supervision.
- Adults should insert and remove the sharp metal blade in the food processor—and wash it, too.
- Make sure the blender is not too full and that the top is on tight. Hold your hand on the top before switching on the motor.
- Don't let kids put rubber spatulas or their fingers into the bowl of an electric mixer while it's running.
- Turn pan handles toward the back of the stove to prevent knocking them.
- Have thick oven mitts and pot holders nearby.
- Never run or play in the kitchen while prepping food and cooking.
- Keep a fire extinguisher in the kitchen and teach your kids how to use it.

CHOICES

You probably won't want to try a new recipe every night, but you might want to leaf through the following pages with your kids and let them pick out a few dishes that appeal to one or another of them. Kids like the freedom that comes with making choices, whether it's choosing what to eat for dinner or what toppings to put on their tacos or pizza. They will enjoy planning some of the family's upcoming meals, too.

Once you've decided on some recipes, ask the kids to check the pantry and refrigerator before you make a shopping list together. Let them help you shop and, if they are old enough, to find specific items in the supermarket. If you have a garden or pots of herbs at home, let them harvest what they will need for a particular dish and encourage them to smell and taste the fragrant leaves and appreciate that perfectly ripe tomato or pepper. Involving them in the entire process adds to the excitement and appreciation of cooking and sets them on the path to making healthful choices for themselves when they're not at home.

This is the idea behind *The Family Kitchen*. So roll up your sleeves and get started!

breakfast

classic popovers ✳ bursting blueberry pancakes with blueberry maple syrup ✳ easy apple pancake ✳ raisin and apricot breakfast cookies ✳ individual zucchini and cheddar frittatas ✳ steel-cut oatmeal with dried fruit and cinnamon cream ✳ honey nut granola ✳ irish soda bread ✳ hash brown fritters ✳ pear and ricotta blintzes with raspberry-maple butter sauce

The idea of skipping breakfast is totally foreign to me, regardless of how much or little time we have in the morning to connect. There may be little time to cook breakfast during the week, but on weekend mornings, when my kids wander into the kitchen and see the flour canister and egg carton on the counter, they quickly perk up with two of their favorite questions: "What are you making?" and "Can I help?" This is the first meal many parents and children cook together and breakfast recipes, like dessert recipes, are learning grounds for early culinary skills. Plain and simple, kids *like* breakfast foods and are usually excited to help with the measuring and prepping. The recipes are easy and fast and as such appeal to kids. Weekends are perfect for teaching your kids how to make pancakes, bread, and egg dishes. You have time, and the extra effort is always well worth it. Plus, kids love the flavors and textures of breakfast foods: mild, sweet, and soothing with just a little crunch to propel them into the day ahead.

classic popovers

This has to be one of my kids' favorite recipes, in large part because they love the anticipation of the puffy, golden rolls emerging from the oven. We like them for breakfast but they're good at any meal. The fact that they are hollow does not detract from their homey deliciousness. It somehow enhances it. The batter is really easy to mix and yet the results are so dramatic. Be sure to caution the kids not to open the oven but instead to watch the magic rising through the oven window; if the heat escapes during baking, the popovers will deflate. And where's the fun in that?

Preheat the oven to 425°F. Generously brush 9 cups of a muffin tin with 2 tablespoons of the melted butter.

In a medium bowl, whisk together the milk, flour, and eggs until smooth. Stir in the remaining 2 tablespoons butter.

Fill each muffin cup halfway with batter. Bake for 30 minutes, without opening the oven. The popovers will puff up in the oven so that they crown dramatically over the rims of the muffin cups and turn golden brown. Serve immediately.

MAKES 9 POPOVERS

4 tablespoons (1/2 stick) unsalted butter, melted
1 cup milk
1 cup all-purpose flour
2 large eggs

Call the Kids
- Butter the muffin tin
- Measure and pour the milk
- Measure the flour
- Whisk the batter
- Pour or spoon the batter into the muffin cups

bursting blueberry pancakes with blueberry maple syrup

My kids and I make these just about every Sunday morning. We like these pancakes that much, and like all pancakes, they are easy to mix. Here, I add blueberries, my first choice, but because my husband prefers his pancakes plain and one of my sons likes them with chocolate chips, we sometimes divide the batter and customize it for each family member. The same is true of the syrup. You can go with plain maple syrup, but for me, adding blueberries to it makes it special because I remember as a kid how much I loved flavored syrups at the International House of Pancakes.

1 cup milk

4 tablespoons ($1/2$ stick) unsalted butter

2 large eggs

$1^1/_4$ cups all-purpose flour

1 tablespoon plus 2 teaspoons sugar

4 teaspoons baking powder

Pinch of salt

$2^1/_2$ cups fresh or frozen blueberries

Flavorless vegetable oil spray

Blueberry Maple Syrup (recipe follows)

Call the Kids

- Stir together the cooled milk and eggs
- Measure the flour and sugar
- Whisk the dry ingredients
- Mix the batter
- Measure and mix the syrup ingredients

USE YOUR JUDGMENT

- Ladle the batter onto the hot griddle

In a small saucepan, heat the milk and butter over low heat until the butter melts. Stir to combine and then set aside to cool to room temperature.

In a large bowl, lightly beat the eggs with a fork. Add the cooled milk mixture and beat well.

In another mixing bowl, combine the flour, sugar, baking powder, and salt and whisk to mix well. Gradually add to the milk and eggs and stir with a wooden spoon just until the batter is combined. Do not overmix. Stir in the blueberries.

Lightly spray a griddle or large skillet with flavorless vegetable oil spray and heat over medium-high heat. When hot, ladle the batter onto the griddle in about $1/_4$-cup amounts, leaving room for the pancakes to spread. Cook for about 1 minute, or until bubbles on each pancake break and remain open. Turn and cook for 15 to 30 seconds longer, or until lightly browned. Serve immediately with Blueberry Maple Syrup.

SERVES 6; MAKES 24 PANCAKES

blueberry maple syrup

In a small saucepan, heat the blueberries and syrup together over medium heat for 3 to 4 minutes, or until the berries just begin to open.

Strain through a mesh sieve, forcing the solids through with the back of a spoon or ladle. Stir in the lemon juice and serve warm.

MAKES 1 CUP

1 cup fresh or frozen blueberries
$^{1}/_{2}$ cup pure maple syrup
1 teaspoon fresh lemon juice

TIP When fresh berries seem to be nearing the end of their season, freeze them in small plastic freezer bags. You can add frozen berries to pancake or muffin batter without thawing them; frozen berries don't bleed into the batter and are less apt to get mushy.

easy apple pancake

My grandmother taught me to make this simple breakfast dish and ever since, I've indulged myself time and again. It's more of a crepe than a pancake—there's just enough batter to hold the apples together—and like crepes, is better cooked one at a time.

2 apples
2 tablespoons unsalted butter
2 large eggs
$^1/_4$ cup milk
$^1/_4$ cup all-purpose flour
$^1/_2$ teaspoon ground cinnamon
Pure maple syrup
Confectioners' sugar

Call the Kids

- Whisk together the eggs, milk, flour, and cinnamon
  USE YOUR JUDGMENT
- Flip the pancake

Preheat the oven to 200°F.

Peel, core, and thinly slice the apples.

In an 8-inch sauté pan, melt 1 tablespoon of the butter over medium-high heat until it begins to bubble. Spread half the apple slices evenly on the bottom of the pan, reduce the heat to medium, and cook for 2 to 3 minutes, or until they begin to wilt.

Meanwhile, in a bowl, whisk together the eggs, milk, flour, and cinnamon until smooth. Pour half of the egg mixture over the apple slices, cover the pan, and cook for 2 to 3 minutes, or until the pancake begins to set up and the sides look dry.

Using a flexible spatula, flip the pancake over. Cook for another minute, and then slide onto an oven-safe plate and keep warm in the oven while you make the second pancake.

Serve with syrup and confectioners' sugar.

SERVES 2

raisin and apricot breakfast cookies

As someone who loves sweets, I like the idea of a healthful cookie for breakfast. Prunes or apple-sauce, rather than butter, make these moist. And yet, my kids gobble these up. In fact, when I talked to my daughter, Remy, about this book, she urged me to include this recipe. "You have to put them in the book, Mom. They are soooo good!" I agree.

Preheat the oven to 350°F. Lightly grease 2 baking sheets with butter.

In a large bowl, combine the flour, oats, sugar, baking soda, baking powder, cinnamon, and salt. Add the prune purée, orange juice, melted butter, egg whites, and vanilla. Mix with a wooden spoon until blended. Stir in the raisins and apricots.

For each cookie, scoop 2 generous tablespoons of dough from the bowl and drop onto the baking sheets. Bake for 10 to 11 minutes, until just set and lightly browned around the edges. Do not overbake.

Transfer the cookies to wire racks to cool. Store in an airtight container for up to 3 days.

MAKES 18 COOKIES

Unsalted butter

2 cups all-purpose flour

1¼ cups old-fashioned rolled oats

1 cup packed light brown sugar

1½ teaspoons baking soda

½ teaspoon baking powder

¾ teaspoon ground cinnamon

¼ teaspoon salt

¼ cup store-bought prune purée or applesauce

¼ cup orange juice

3 tablespoons unsalted butter, melted

3 large egg whites

1 teaspoon pure vanilla extract

⅓ cup raisins

¼ cup chopped dried apricots

Call the Kids
- Grease the baking sheets
- Measure the flour, oats, and sugar
- Measure the prune purée and orange juice
- Measure the raisins and apricots
- Stir the batter together by hand
- Drop cookies onto the baking sheets

individual zucchini and cheddar frittatas

These look so appealing when they come out of the oven that the kids snap them up. Kids like to make and eat something that is small and self-contained, and these little frittatas fit the bill. Although I first started making these for very grown-up brunches, they are easy to make when you're learning to cook. Serve the mildly cheesy frittatas with bacon, sausage, or potatoes—or on their own.

Flavorless vegetable oil spray
2 tablespoons olive oil
$1^1/_2$ medium zucchini, shredded on the
    large holes of a box grater
2 shallots, thinly sliced
$^3/_4$ teaspoon salt
Freshly ground pepper
7 large eggs
$^2/_3$ cup half-and-half
$^1/_2$ cup shredded white Cheddar cheese
$^1/_2$ teaspoon chopped fresh thyme
    leaves

Call the Kids

- Spray the muffin cups with vegetable oil spray
- Grate the zucchini with a box grater
- Measure the half-and-half
- Mix the zucchini and shallots
- Mix together the egg mixture
- Divide the zucchini mixture among the muffin cups
- Spoon the egg mixture over the zucchini

Preheat the oven to 375°F. Generously spray 12 cups of a muffin tin with flavorless vegetable oil spray.

In a medium sauté pan, heat the oil over medium-high heat until just shimmering. Add the zucchini and shallots and sauté for 3 to 4 minutes, or until wilted and soft. Pour off or drain any excess moisture. Season with $^1/_4$ teaspoon of the salt and about $^1/_8$ teaspoon pepper.

In a large bowl, whisk together the eggs, half-and-half, Cheddar cheese, thyme, and the remaining $^1/_2$ teaspoon salt. Season with a few grinds of pepper.

Divide the zucchini mixture among the muffin cups. Top each cup with the egg mixture, dividing it equally among the cups. Bake for about 20 minutes, or until puffy, golden brown, and just set.

Run a dull kitchen knife around the outside of each frittata and remove. Serve immediately.

MAKES 12 FRITTATAS

NOTE: Similar frittatas can be made with cooked spinach, mushrooms, grilled vegetables, and ham. Substitute Gruyère cheese for the Cheddar. Extras can be wrapped and refrigerated, and then reheated for about 1 minute in the microwave.

steel-cut oatmeal with dried fruit and cinnamon cream

I love the hearty texture of steel-cut oatmeal and how it fills you up in the morning. When you add dried fruits, it's even more satisfying, healthful, and hearty. The cinnamon dresses up the whipped cream and the whipped cream dresses up the whole thing. My kids think such an indulgence on top of their oatmeal is awesome at breakfast.

2 cups milk

2 cups water

1 cup Irish steel-cut oats

Pinch of salt

$^1/_2$ cup heavy cream

2 teaspoons confectioners' sugar

$^1/_4$ teaspoon ground cinnamon

$^1/_2$ cup dried fruit, such as raisins, chopped dried apricots, and dried cherries

4 tablespoons honey

In a medium saucepan, bring the milk and water to a boil over high heat. Stir in the oats and salt and return to a boil. Reduce the heat and simmer over medium-low heat for about 30 minutes, stirring occasionally, until the oats absorb the liquid and are soft.

Meanwhile, in a medium bowl and using a wire whisk, whip the cream, confectioners' sugar, and cinnamon together until the mixture forms soft peaks.

Remove the cooked oatmeal from the heat and distribute among 4 serving bowls. Sprinkle each bowl with dried fruit and drizzle with honey. Top with a dollop of the cinnamon cream and serve immediately.

SERVES 4

Call the Kids

- Measure the milk and water
- Measure the oats
- Measure the cream
- Measure the dried fruits
- Whip the cream
- Top the oatmeal with fruit, honey, and whipped cream

USE YOUR JUDGMENT

- Stir the oats while they cook

honey nut granola

I've been making this granola for years. It's the same mixture we sell at the store and believe me, we sell a lot of it! It's versatile, easy, crunchy, healthful, and really, really good. We eat it mixed with yogurt or milk or sprinkled over ice cream.

Preheat the oven to 325°F.

In a small saucepan, cook the honey, brown sugar, and vanilla over medium heat, stirring occasionally, until the sugar melts.

In a medium bowl, combine the oats, sunflower seeds, almonds, walnuts, and coconut. Add the sugar mixture and toss until the granola is evenly coated.

Lightly grease a baking sheet with the vegetable oil spray or butter. Spread out the mixture in an even layer and bake for 25 minutes, stirring with a long-handled wooden spoon once or twice during this time.

Remove the granola from the oven, and let it cool to room temperature in the pan. Break the granola into chunks and store in a sealed plastic bag or lidded container for up to 2 weeks.

MAKES ABOUT 7 CUPS

$1/2$ cup honey
$1/2$ cup packed dark brown sugar
$1 1/2$ teaspoons pure vanilla extract
2 cups old-fashioned rolled oats
1 cup shelled sunflower seeds
1 cup sliced or slivered almonds
1 cup chopped walnuts
1 cup sweetened shredded coconut
Flavorless vegetable oil spray or
  unsalted butter

Call the Kids

- Measure the brown sugar
- Measure the oats, sunflower seeds, almonds, walnuts, and coconut
- Mix the oats, sunflower seeds, almonds, walnuts, and coconut
- Toss the granola
- Grease the baking sheet
- Spread the granola on the baking sheet
- Break the cooled granola into chunks

irish soda bread

Nothing beats homemade bread, warm from the oven, spread with melting butter, especially on a blustery March day. While we make this easy quick bread every Saint Patrick's Day, it's no stranger in our house at other times of the year. Quick breads are a satisfying alternative to yeast breads, which, let's face it, require more patience. Not always a strong suit with my kids!

4 cups all-purpose flour, plus more for kneading

1 tablespoon baking powder

1 teaspoon baking soda

1 teaspoon salt

4 tablespoons ($^1\!/_2$ stick) cold unsalted butter, cut into pieces

1 cup dried currants

$^1\!/_3$ cup honey

1$^1\!/_2$ teaspoons caraway seeds

2 teaspoons finely grated orange zest

1$^1\!/_2$ cups buttermilk (see Note)

$^1\!/_4$ cup orange juice

Call the Kids

- Measure the flour
- Measure the currants and caraway seeds
- Measure the buttermilk and orange juice
- Mix the dough
- Knead the dough
- Form the loaf

Preheat the oven to 350°F.

In the bowl of an electric mixer fitted with the paddle attachment, combine the flour, baking powder, baking soda, and salt. Mix on low speed to combine.

Raise the speed to medium low and add the butter, a piece or two at a time, until all of the butter has been incorporated and the mixture is crumbly. This will take 4 to 5 minutes.

Add the currants, honey, caraway seeds, and orange zest and mix until evenly distributed. Add the buttermilk and orange juice and mix just until combined. Do not overmix.

Turn the dough out onto a floured work surface and knead a few times, adding more flour if the dough is too sticky, until it is smooth and cohesive. Form the dough into a smooth, round loaf and transfer to a nonstick baking sheet. Make a crosshatch design on the top of the loaf, using a blunt knife or fork to break the skin of the dough at about 1-inch intervals. Sprinkle with a little flour. Bake for about 45 minutes, or until the loaf is set and sounds hollow when tapped on the bottom. Let the bread cool on a rack. Serve warm or at room temperature.

MAKES 1 LOAF

NOTE: Because fresh buttermilk is not a staple in most houses, I keep buttermilk powder in the cupboard, which is easily reconstituted with water, following the instructions on the box. I find I use it more than you might think for quick breads, muffins, and scones. You can buy it at whole-food markets. Of course, you can always sour milk to use as a replacement for buttermilk. Add 1 tablespoon of fresh lemon juice or white distilled vinegar for every cup of milk.

hash brown fritters

Here is my favorite way to use leftover potatoes. In fact, these hash browns are so good, I often bake extra potatoes the night before so that I can make these in the morning. We started making these fritters at Aux Délices for breakfast—and sure, they take a little more time than other hash browns, but they are terrific, and hash browns always make a weekend breakfast seem more complete.

Preheat the oven to 350°F.

Put the potatoes on a baking sheet and bake for 45 to 55 minutes, or until tender when pricked with a fork. Remove from the oven and cool.

Cut the potatoes in half, scoop out the flesh, and crumble it into a medium bowl.

In a medium sauté pan, heat 1 tablespoon of the oil over medium-high heat and add the bell pepper, onion, and scallion. Sauté, stirring occasionally, for about 5 minutes, or until the vegetables are softened and translucent. Add to the potatoes and stir to mix.

Add the egg and flour to the mixture and season with salt and pepper. Mix well.

In the same sauté pan, heat the remaining $1/2$ cup oil over medium heat until it shimmers. Put heaping tablespoons of the fritter mixture into the hot oil and press lightly with the back of a spoon so that they are about $1/2$ inch thick. Cook for about 2 minutes on each side, or until golden brown. Drain on paper towels. Sprinkle with salt and serve hot.

MAKES 14 TO 16 FRITTERS

3 large baking potatoes (about
   $1^3/_4$ pounds), washed
$1/2$ cup plus 1 tablespoon canola oil
$1/2$ red bell pepper, seeded and chopped
$1/4$ small white onion, chopped
1 scallion, trimmed and thinly sliced
1 large egg
$3^1/_2$ tablespoons all-purpose flour
Salt and freshly ground pepper

Call the Kids
- Scoop out the cooled potato flesh
- Mix the vegetables with the potatoes
- Add the egg and flour to the potatoes

USE YOUR JUDGMENT
- Form the fritters in the pan

pear and ricotta blintzes with raspberry-maple butter sauce

Blintzes, made by filling and rolling crepes, are a nice change from pancakes, and I've found that kids love to make the crepes. The smooth cheese and pear filling I use here is sweet enough to appeal to the kids without being too cloying for the adults. The crepes can be made ahead of time and frozen, and even the blintzes can be filled, rolled, and refrigerated a day before serving.

4 ripe, firm pears, peeled, cut
   lengthwise in half, and cored
6 ounces cream cheese, at room
   temperature
1/3 cup sugar
2 large eggs
1 teaspoon grated lemon zest
1 teaspoon grated orange zest
1 teaspoon pure vanilla extract
One 15-ounce container ricotta cheese
Unsalted butter
Debra's Crepes (recipe follows)
Raspberry-Maple Butter Sauce (recipe
   follows)

Preheat the oven to 325°F.

Put the pears, cut sides down, on a baking sheet and bake for 45 minutes, or until the pears are a little softer and have released some juices. Let the pears cool on the baking sheet, and then cut into small pieces.

In the bowl of an electric mixer fitted with the paddle attachment and set on medium-high speed, beat the cream cheese and sugar until smooth. Add the eggs one at a time, and then beat in the zests and vanilla.

Using a wooden spoon or spatula, fold the ricotta cheese and pears into the cream cheese mixture. Cover and refrigerate for at least 1 hour and up to 2 hours.

Preheat the oven to 375°F. and butter a 13 x 9 x 2-inch pan.

Place a crepe on a work surface. Spoon 1/4 cup of the filling onto the center of the crepe and fold the bottom up and over the filling. Fold in the sides and roll the crepe into a neat package. Lay it seam side down in the buttered dish. Repeat with the remaining filling and crepes to make 14 blintzes.

Cover the pan with foil and bake for about 35 minutes, or until the blintzes are heated through. Serve with Raspberry-Maple Butter Sauce.

SERVES 6 TO 8; MAKES 14 BLINTZES

Call the Kids

- Measure the milk, flour, and sugar for the crepes
- Mix the batter
- Rip sheets of wax paper to put between crepes
- Dice the pears with a blunt knife
- Mix the filling for the blintzes
- Fill and roll the crepes into blintzes
- Measure the maple syrup, cinnamon, and butter for the sauce
- Stir the maple syrup and raspberries together

USE YOUR JUDGMENT
- Flip the crepes in the pan

debra's crepes

In a large bowl using a hand-held electric blender or wire whisk, blend together the milk, eggs, flour, melted butter, sugar, and salt. If the batter seems thin, add more flour. It should be the consistency of heavy cream. When smooth, set aside to rest for at least 30 minutes and up to 45 minutes.

Heat an 8-inch crepe pan over medium heat for 1 minute, then spray it with vegetable oil spray.

Using a ladle or measuring cup, pour about 1/4 cup of the crepe batter into the pan and tilt it in all directions until the bottom of the pan is evenly coated. Cook for 30 seconds, or until the crepe begins to dry around the edges. Using a thin-edged spatula, turn the crepe and cook the other side for 15 to 20 seconds, or until the crepe is lightly browned.

Remove the crepe from the pan and lay it on a plate while you make the next crepe. Stack the crepes on the plate, separated with sheets of wax paper so that they won't stick together. Cover with a dish towel to keep warm. If not using right away, let the stack of crepes cool, wrap them in plastic wrap, and refrigerate overnight or freeze for up to 1 month.

MAKES 14 CREPES

1 cup whole milk

3 large eggs

About 1/3 cup plus 1 tablespoon
    all-purpose flour

2 tablespoons unsalted butter, melted

1 tablespoon sugar

Pinch of salt

Flavorless vegetable oil spray

TIP Crepes also make delicious desserts. Fill or top them with melted semisweet or bittersweet chocolate, chocolate chips, fudge sauce, caramel sauce, sweetened whipped cream, fresh berries or sliced bananas, peaches, or mangoes, sweetened shaved coconut, or a simple mixture of melted butter and ground cinnamon.

raspberry-maple butter sauce

In a small saucepan, heat the maple syrup and cinnamon together over medium heat until hot.

Lower the heat to low and whisk in the butter, a tablespoon at a time, until incorporated. Simmer the sauce on low heat for 2 to 3 minutes.

Remove the pan from the heat and stir in the raspberries. Serve warm, or cover and set aside until ready to serve. Reheat very gently before serving.

MAKES ABOUT 2 CUPS

1 cup pure maple syrup

3/4 teaspoon ground cinnamon

4 tablespoons (1/2 stick) unsalted butter

1/2 pint fresh raspberries or 8 ounces
    whole frozen, unsweetened
    raspberries, thawed

breakfast in bed

strawberry smoothies ✳ stone fruit salad with honey and lime ✳ scrambled eggs with cheddar and ham ✳ blueberry crumb muffins ✳ fresh berry bismarck

How great is breakfast in bed? Who doesn't like being on the receiving end, or, just as exciting, the planning team for this treat? I put this chapter together to give you and your kids ideas for what to make on Mother's Day, Father's Day, and various birthdays—but breakfast in bed could become a more regular event if your family is game. The recipes are easy enough for the kids to do by themselves or with minimal help from an adult, and not one requires more than a fork and spoon to eat. My kids love setting up the tray and helping whichever parent is on kitchen duty prepare a luxurious morning meal. They even like making breakfast in bed for each other on birthdays and other special occasions.

The kids can pile the blueberry muffins in a basket, pour the smoothies into tall, colorful glasses, or serve the fruit salad in a goblet or pretty bowl. They love carrying the tray into the bedroom, and another can share in the fun by bringing in the muffin-filled basket. If your kids are anything like mine, when the tray filled with food is placed on the bed, they'll scramble up there with you, forks at the ready to sample their handiwork.

strawberry smoothies

Smoothies are a breakfast favorite with everyone, and kids, in particular, like to customize their own, exercise some free choice, and indulge in their creativity! I suggest strawberries for this recipe, but you could use any other fresh or frozen berries you have on hand. In our house we like smoothies with bananas and mangoes. You can mix and match the yogurts, too.

Put strawberries, yogurt, and orange juice in a blender and blend until smooth. Pour into glasses and serve.

SERVES 4; MAKES 3 CUPS

1 pint strawberries, hulled and halved
$^3/_4$ cup vanilla or strawberry yogurt
1 cup orange juice

Call the Kids

- Hull and halve the strawberries with a blunt knife
- Measure the yogurt and orange juice
- Put the ingredients in the blender

stone fruit salad with honey and lime

Tree-ripe peaches, plums, nectarines, and cherries are high-summer treats, and I think teaching kids about seasonal perfection is a valuable lesson: nothing tastes better than fruit picked at the peak of perfection. The squeeze of lime juice and drops of honey heighten the already magnificent flavor.

Cut the nectarines in half and remove the pit. Cut each half into 6 pieces. Repeat for the plums and peaches. Transfer to a mixing bowl, add the cherries, and stir gently to mix.

In a small bowl, stir together the honey and lime juice. Pour over the fruit and toss gently to mix.

Scatter the mint leaves over the fruit salad and serve.

SERVES 6 TO 8

2 ripe nectarines
2 ripe plums
2 ripe peaches
20 cherries, pitted and halved
2 tablespoons honey
Juice of 1 lime, about 2 tablespoons
5 to 6 fresh mint leaves, torn into pieces

Call the Kids

- Pit the cherries with a pitting tool
- Cut the fruit with a blunt knife
- Tear the mint leaves into small pieces
- Mix the dressing
- Toss the salad

scrambled eggs with cheddar and ham

Scrambled eggs are one of the first things everyone learns to make and once you master them, you'll never go hungry! When a beginner figures out that low heat yields the creamiest, softest eggs, even the most impulsive young cook will learn patience. You can leave out the ham or cheese, or both, if your kids prefer. These are something your kids can make from start to finish without any help once they are old enough to man the stove.

4 large eggs

2 tablespoons milk or half-and-half

$1/3$ cup shredded Cheddar cheese

$1/3$ cup chopped thinly sliced ham

1 teaspoon salt

Freshly ground pepper

1 teaspoon unsalted butter

In a medium bowl, whisk together the eggs and milk. Add the cheese, ham, and salt and season with a few grinds of pepper.

In a small sauté pan, melt the butter over low heat. Add the egg mixture and stir continuously, scraping the bottom of the pan, for 3 to 4 minutes, or until the eggs begin to set in small curds and are no longer wet and runny. Serve hot.

SERVES 2

Call the Kids

- Mix together the eggs and milk
- Add the cheese and ham to the eggs
  USE YOUR JUDGMENT
- Stir the eggs in the pan

blueberry crumb muffins

We love to make muffins, which are easy for kids to tackle whether they're making you breakfast in bed or it's a lazy summer morning. In our household, we particularly like blueberry muffins with a crumb topping, but we've made these muffins with strawberries and raspberries in place of blueberries and have been very happy with the results. Eat these warm, without any butter or jam. They are that moist!

Preheat the oven to 375°F. Spray a 12-cup muffin tin with flavorless vegetable oil spray or line the tin with paper liners.

In a mixing bowl, mix together the flour, baking powder, and salt and whisk well.

In the bowl of an electric mixer fitted with the paddle attachment and set on medium-high speed, beat the butter and granulated sugar for 4 to 5 minutes, or until light and fluffy. Add the eggs one at a time, beating after each addition until the egg is incorporated before adding the next one, and then beat in the vanilla.

Add the milk, alternating it with the dry ingredients, in 2 or 3 additions. Do not overmix. Fold in the berries using a spatula.

To make the crumb topping, in the bowl of an electric mixer fitted with the paddle attachment, combine the butter, granulated sugar, dark brown sugar, cinnamon, salt, and flour and mix on medium speed until crumbly.

Spoon the batter into the prepared muffin tin. Top each with a generous tablespoon of the crumb topping. Bake for about 30 minutes, or until golden brown and a toothpick inserted in the center of one comes out clean. Let the muffins cool slightly in the muffin tin set on wire racks before removing.

MAKES 12 MUFFINS

Flavorless vegetable oil spray
2 cups all-purpose flour
2 teaspoons baking powder
1/2 teaspoon salt
1/2 cup (1 stick) unsalted butter
1 cup granulated sugar
2 large eggs
1 teaspoon pure vanilla extract
1/2 cup milk
2 1/2 cups fresh or frozen blueberries

CRUMB TOPPING
6 tablespoons (3/4 stick) unsalted butter
1/4 cup granulated sugar
1/4 cup packed dark brown sugar
3/4 teaspoon ground cinnamon
Pinch of salt
1 1/2 cups all-purpose flour

Call the Kids
- Spray the muffin tin with vegetable oil
- Measure the flour
- Mix the flour, baking powder, and salt
- Measure the sugar
- Beat the butter and sugar
- Add the eggs
- Measure and add the milk
- Fold the blueberries into the batter
- Measure the ingredients for the crumb topping
- Spoon the batter into the tins
- Add the crumb topping

fresh berry bismarck

When I was a child I read a lot of cookbooks, usually those directed at young, novice cooks. While I can't recall where I found a recipe similar to this one, it was one of the first breakfast dishes I learned to make and I have always been fond of it. Not only are bismarcks (which are also called Dutch babies) impressive because they puff up so dramatically in the oven, the topping choices are practically endless and run the gamut from syrup to fresh fruit to confectioners' sugar. I especially like recipes in which the kids have choices.

Preheat the oven to 475°F.

Put the butter in a 10-inch ovenproof sauté pan and heat in the oven until the butter melts and begins to bubble. Watch this carefully so that the butter does not burn.

Meanwhile, in a large bowl and using a wire whisk or hand-held electric mixer, whisk together the flour, milk, eggs, and salt until smooth.

Pour the batter into the sauté pan and return to the oven for about 12 minutes, or until the batter is puffy and golden brown.

Slide the puffed bismarck onto a serving plate. Drizzle with maple syrup, fresh berries, and confectioners' sugar. Cut in half and serve immediately.

SERVES 2

2 tablespoons unsalted butter
$^1/_2$ cup all-purpose flour
$^1/_2$ cup milk
2 large eggs
Pinch of salt
Pure maple syrup
Fresh raspberries, blueberries, or
    strawberries
Confectioners' sugar
Special equipment: a 10-inch ovenproof
    sauté pan

Call the Kids
- Measure the flour and milk
- Whisk the batter
- Garnish the bismarck with syrup, berries, and confectioners' sugar

lunch at home

grilled prosciutto, provolone, and tomato sandwich ❈ spinach salad with dried cherries, almonds, and blue cheese ❈ herbed egg salad stuffed pitas ❈ croque monsieur ❈ curried chicken salad with apples and currants ❈ tuna, pasta, and celery salad ❈ garden vegetable soup with pesto ❈ spicy chicken tortilla soup ❈ fresh mayonnaise

spinach salad with dried cherries, almonds, and blue cheese

Baby spinach salad is a great favorite with most kids because of its mildness. When you add sweet dried cherries to the mix, the combination of ingredients is fantastic. If you prefer, substitute goat cheese for the blue cheese, or omit the cheese altogether.

VINAIGRETTE

2 tablespoons red wine vinegar

1 tablespoon finely chopped shallot

$1/4$ teaspoon salt

$1/4$ cup extra-virgin olive oil

Freshly ground pepper

SALAD

8 ounces baby spinach leaves, rinsed
   and dried

1 apple, cored, peeled, and thinly sliced

$1/2$ cup dried cherries

$1/2$ cup sliced almonds

$1/2$ cup crumbled blue cheese

In a small bowl, whisk together the vinegar, shallot, and salt until the salt is dissolved. Slowly whisk in the oil. Season to taste with pepper. Set aside until needed. Whisk just before using.

In a large bowl, toss together the spinach, apple, dried cherries, and almonds. Toss the salad with enough dressing to wet the leaves lightly, and then gently stir in the blue cheese.

TIP When you make a vinaigrette, first dissolve the salt in the vinegar. Salt does not easily dissolve in oil, so if it's already mixed with the vinegar before the oil is added, its flavor will disperse more evenly in the finished dressing.

SERVES 4

Call the Kids

- Measure the oil
- Mix the dressing
- Rinse and spin dry the spinach
- Peel the apple with a hand-held peeler
- Measure the cherries and almonds
- Toss the salad

herbed egg salad stuffed pitas

This is a nice change from more ordinary egg salad. The dill adds fresh flavor and it's always fun to make sandwiches with pita pockets, which are a nice change from two slices of bread. Kids like them, and the pockets make it easy to personalize the sandwiches by adding your own touches such as grated cheese, chopped red onion, grated carrots, or sliced cucumbers.

In a medium bowl, combine the mayonnaise, dill, mustard, chives, and lemon zest. Add the grated eggs and toss gently. Season with salt and pepper.

Cut each pita in half and open the pockets. Place a slice of tomato into each pita, and then stuff the pocket with egg salad. Garnish each sandwich with alfalfa sprouts.

SERVES 4

3 tablespoons mayonnaise
2 tablespoons chopped fresh dill
1 teaspoon Dijon mustard
1 teaspoon chopped fresh chives
$1/4$ teaspoon grated lemon zest
6 hard-boiled eggs, peeled and grated
Salt and freshly ground pepper
4 whole pitas, each about 4 inches in
  diameter
1 large tomato, cored and sliced
Alfalfa sprouts

Call the Kids
- Grate the eggs
- Mix the dressing
- Stuff the pitas

croque monsieur

Here's an easy home version of the classic French sandwich. Kids love any kind of grilled sandwich and especially like this one with mild Gruyère melting into the thinly sliced ham.

2 tablespoons mayonnaise

¾ teaspoon Dijon mustard

8 slices white bread

4 thin slices ham

8 thin slices Gruyère cheese
  (6 to 8 ounces)

2 tablespoons unsalted butter, melted

Call the Kids

- Stir the mayonnaise and mustard together
- Spread the bread with the mayonnaise-mustard mixture
- Lay the ham and cheese slices on the bread
- Brush the melted butter on the sandwiches

In a small bowl, stir together 1 tablespoon of the mayonnaise and the mustard. Spread evenly over 4 slices of the bread. Arrange a slice of ham and a slice of Gruyère on each piece of bread.

Put the remaining 4 slices of bread on top of the sandwiches. Brush the outside of both slices of bread with the melted butter.

Preheat an indoor grill or heat a nonstick grill pan over medium-high heat.

Grill for 2 to 3 minutes on each side or until the bread is lightly browned on both sides and there are nice-looking grill marks on the bread. Using a large spatula, transfer the sandwiches to a broiling tray or cookie sheet.

Preheat the broiler.

Spread the top of the sandwiches with the remaining tablespoon mayonnaise and top with the 4 remaining slices Gruyère, being sure to cover the crusts of the bread.

Broil, cheese side up, for 1 to 2 minutes, or until bubbly and golden brown. Serve hot.

SERVES 4

curried chicken salad with apples and currants

When I started making this with my kids, I added just a little curry powder and balanced it with the sweetness of the apples. Cut back on the curry powder if you don't think it will go over in your house. Once your kids develop a taste for curry, they will love this.

In a medium bowl, combine the mayonnaise and the curry powder. Add the chicken, apple, onion, currants, parsley, lemon juice, salt, and pepper and toss gently.

SERVES 4 TO 6

$2/3$ cup Fresh Mayonnaise (page 51), or store-bought

1 tablespoon curry powder, or to taste

4 cups cooked chicken breast, cubed (about $1^1/4$ pounds)

$1/2$ Granny Smith apple, peeled, cored, and sliced

$1/2$ cup diced white onion (about $1/2$ medium onion)

$1/4$ cup currants or raisins

$1/4$ cup chopped fresh flat-leaf parsley leaves

1 tablespoon fresh lemon juice

$1/2$ teaspoon salt

$1/4$ teaspoon cracked black pepper

Call the Kids

- Measure the mayonnaise
- Peel the apple with a hand-held peeler
- Measure the currants or raisins
- Pull the parsley leaves from the stems
- Mix the mayonnaise and curry powder
- Add the remaining ingredients to the mayonnaise mixture

tuna, pasta, and celery salad

When I lived in New York City years ago, my apartment was across the street from Grace's Market-place, a famous spot for gourmet food items and takeout. I discovered a salad very similar to this one there and soon found myself ducking into the store several times a week for a small container. I make this with homemade mayonnaise and while I have nothing against store-bought brands, the "real thing" makes a big difference in flavor here. I think my kids like this salad because it's so straight-forward, with recognizable, familiar ingredients.

8 ounces elbow macaroni

One 6-ounce can tuna packed in water, drained

3 celery ribs, thinly sliced on the bias

1/3 cup Fresh Mayonnaise (page 51), or store-bought

Salt and freshly ground pepper

Cook the macaroni in boiling salted water according to the package directions. Drain and cool.

In a medium bowl, mix together the tuna, celery, and mayonnaise. Season to taste with salt and pepper.

Add the macaroni to the bowl and toss well. Serve.

SERVES 4

Call the Kids

- Drain the tuna
- Measure the mayonnaise
- Mix the tuna, celery, and mayonnaise
- Toss the pasta with the tuna salad

garden vegetable soup with pesto

When going through my grandmother's recipe file one day, I came across this soup, handwritten in her familiar script. She was a great cook and, more than anyone else, inspired me to find my way around a kitchen. I was thrilled to find a family recipe that I knew the kids could help with and which they would like because of the soup's mild, light flavor and variety of vegetables. I have improved on my grandmother's recipe by adding pesto for flavor and fragrance.

In a large soup pot, bring the stock, carrot, onion, and garlic to a boil over medium-high heat. Reduce the heat and simmer for 10 to 12 minutes, until the carrots are tender.

Add the canned and fresh beans, tomatoes, zucchini, and spaghetti and simmer for another 10 minutes, stirring occasionally. Add the salt and season to taste with pepper.

Meanwhile, in the bowl of a food processor fitted with the metal blade, combine the basil, cheese, and olive oil and process until smooth.

Just before serving, stir the basil pesto into the soup and ladle into bowls.

SERVES 6 TO 8

1 1/2 quarts chicken or vegetable stock or low-sodium broth
1 medium carrot, peeled and diced
1/2 large onion, diced
2 garlic cloves, thinly sliced
1/2 pound canned cannellini beans, rinsed and drained
1/4 pound fresh green beans, trimmed and cut into 1/2-inch pieces
2 large tomatoes, peeled, seeded, and diced
1 medium zucchini, diced
2 ounces spaghetti, broken into 1-inch pieces
2 teaspoons salt
Freshly ground pepper
1/2 cup torn fresh basil leaves
1/2 cup freshly grated Parmesan cheese
1/2 cup extra-virgin olive oil

Call the Kids
- Peel the carrots with a hand-held peeler
- Rinse and drain the canned beans
- Break up the spaghetti
- Tear up the basil
- Stir the soup

USE YOUR JUDGMENT
- Cut the other vegetables
- Mix the pesto in the food processor

spicy chicken tortilla soup

We used to buy this soup at a local Mexican takeout shop and I so enjoyed it I started making it myself. I like all the components, from the corn to the chicken to the kick provided by the jalapeños. We all like the crunchy fried tortilla topping and the coolness of the avocado relish, which is also great on its own with tortilla or pita chips. If you're pressed for time, substitute tortilla chips for the fried tortilla topping.

2 cups vegetable oil

Twelve 6-inch corn tortillas

2 tablespoons olive oil

$1/2$ large white onion, finely diced

1 pound plum tomatoes, seeded and
   diced

3 large jalapeños, seeded and
   finely diced

1 large carrot, peeled and finely diced

1 large green bell pepper, seeded and
   finely diced

$1/2$ teaspoon dried oregano

$1/4$ teaspoon red pepper flakes

8 cups chicken stock or low-sodium
   broth

$1^{1}/2$ cups cooked shredded chicken
   breast

$1^{1}/2$ cups fresh or frozen and thawed
   corn kernels

Salt

Avocado Relish (recipe follows)

Pour the vegetable oil into a large, heavy pot and heat over medium-high heat until a deep-frying thermometer registers 350°F.

Cut the tortillas in half, and then slice into $1/2$-inch-wide strips. Fry the tortilla strips in batches, so as not to overcrowd the pot, for $1^{1}/2$ to $2^{1}/2$ minutes, or until golden brown. Using tongs, remove from the oil and drain on paper towels. Reserve for garnish.

In another large, heavy pot, heat the olive oil over medium-high heat until almost smoking. Add the onion, tomatoes, jalapeños, carrot, bell pepper, oregano, and pepper flakes and sauté, stirring occasionally, for 5 to 6 minutes. Add the chicken stock, chicken, and corn and season to taste with salt. Bring the soup to a boil.

Crush half of the tortilla strips and add to the boiling soup. Ladle the soup into bowls and garnish with avocado relish and the remaining crispy tortilla strips.

SERVES 10

Call the Kids
- Peel the carrot with a hand-held peeler
- Measure the stock
- Shred the chicken
- Add the vegetables to the pot
- Mix the avocado relish
  USE YOUR JUDGMENT
- Stir the soup

avocado relish

Combine the avocados, tomato, onion, jalapeños, lime juice, and salt in a small bowl and stir to mix. Adjust the seasoning if necessary.

MAKES ABOUT 1 3/4 CUPS

2 ripe avocados, pitted, peeled, and
   finely diced
1 medium tomato, cored, seeded, and
   finely diced
1/2 large onion, finely diced
2 jalapeños, seeded and minced
2 tablespoons fresh lime juice
2 teaspoons salt

fresh mayonnaise

While I am a big fan of high-quality store-bought mayonnaise, there is nothing like the fresh, delicate flavor of homemade. Once you taste the difference, you'll be a true believer, too. It can be whipped up in less than five minutes in a blender. Like any homemade mayonnaise, this is made with raw egg yolks, so if you have any concerns about using them, reach for a jar of pasteurized mayonnaise instead!

In a blender or the bowl of a food processor fitted with a metal blade, process the yolks for about 1 minute. With the motor running, slowly add the olive oil in a very fine stream until the mayonnaise begins to emulsify.

As it thickens, add a few drops of water to loosen the texture, up to 2 tablespoons if necessary. Add the lemon juice and season with salt and pepper.

Transfer the mayonnaise to a glass or plastic container with a tight-fitting lid. Refrigerate for up to 1 week.

MAKES ABOUT 1 CUP

2 large egg yolks
3/4 cup olive oil
1 to 2 tablespoons water
Juice of 1/2 lemon, or to taste
Sea salt and freshly ground pepper

Call the Kids
USE YOUR JUDGMENT
- Blend the eggs
- Add the olive oil
- Add the water
- Add the lemon juice
- Season to taste

snow days

double hot chocolate ❋ homemade marshmallows ❋ pear and dried cherry cobbler ❋ grandma's old-fashioned bread ❋ indian pudding ❋ gray's cinnamon jelly doughnuts

What kid doesn't like to hear those words, "No school today!"? There's really nothing like the cozy feeling of a snow day. Everything stops for a few hours, no one leaves the house (except to venture out into the snowy wonderland), and you can relish the idea of being confined to home and hearth for an entire day! What better excuse to take on a time-consuming kitchen task with the kids, such as making yeast bread or doughnuts? Or to make a sweet, luscious dessert such as Indian Pudding or a fruit-filled cobbler? And when the children come in from the sledding hill, they'll love real hot chocolate, especially if they've helped you make some marshmallows before heading out.

double hot chocolate

This is the real thing: hot chocolate made with real milk, real chocolate, and real cocoa—not hot water and a powdered mix. You can't beat this, and if you float a homemade marshmallow on top, this hot chocolate becomes extra special!

In a small saucepan, stir together the milk, chocolate, cocoa powder, and sugar. Heat over medium heat until hot but not boiling, stirring occasionally.

Pour into mugs and serve topped with marshmallows, if desired.

SERVES 2

2 cups milk
1 ounce semisweet chocolate, chopped
1 tablespoon unsweetened cocoa
   powder
1 tablespoon sugar
Homemade Marshmallows (page 56),
   optional

Call the Kids
- Measure the milk
- Combine the milk, chocolate, cocoa, and sugar in the cool pan
- Top the cocoa with marshmallows or whipped cream

homemade marshmallows

It's true. I actually make my own marshmallows and my kids were thrilled to discover they don't always come out of a bag. Homemade marshmallows are lighter and fluffier than store-bought, and it's this texture that gets high points from most people. Kids can't do the hot sugar work, but they can help along the way, and young and old love eating these.

$2^1/_2$ tablespoons unflavored gelatin
   (1 package)
1 cup cool water
2 large egg whites, at room temperature
1 teaspoon pure vanilla extract, or
   $^1/_2$ vanilla bean, split lengthwise
   and scraped
2 cups granulated sugar
$^1/_2$ cup light corn syrup
Flavorless vegetable oil spray
Confectioners' sugar

Call the Kids
- Measure the water and sugar
- Mix the gelatin with the water
- Whip the egg whites
- Dust the pan with confectioners' sugar
- Dust the marshmallows with confectioners' sugar

In a small bowl, dissolve the gelatin in $^1/_2$ cup of the cool water.

In the bowl of an electric mixer, combine the egg whites and vanilla. Set aside.

In a deep, heavy saucepan, combine the remaining $^1/_2$ cup cool water, the granulated sugar, and the corn syrup. Bring to a boil over medium-high heat, and cook until the syrup reaches 240°F. on a candy thermometer, or the soft ball stage. (To test for the soft ball stage if you don't have a thermometer, drizzle $^1/_4$ teaspoon of the boiling syrup into a cup of cold water. If a soft ball remains in the bottom of the cup, the syrup is ready.)

Meanwhile, when the syrup reaches about 210°F., begin beating the egg whites and vanilla on medium-high speed with the whisk attachment. Beat until stiff but not dry. Alternatively, put the whites and vanilla in a clean, dry mixing bowl and whisk by hand with a wire whisk until stiff but not dry. The goal is to have the egg whites reach stiff peaks when the syrup is cooked. If the whites reach stiff peaks before the syrup is cooked, turn off the mixer until the syrup is ready.

When the sugar syrup reaches 240°F., immediately add the gelatin and water mixture to the syrup and stir to mix. Take care; it will bubble up high in the pan, so make sure the saucepan is deeper and larger than you might think you need.

With the mixer speed on medium low, pour the hot syrup into the whites and beat for 2 to 3 minutes until combined.

Pour into an 8-inch-square pan that has been lightly sprayed with vegetable oil spray and dusted with confectioners' sugar. Spread evenly and dust the top with more confectioners' sugar. Refrigerate for 1 to 2 hours until set. When ready to serve, cut into squares with a hot knife.

MAKES 4 DOZEN MARSHMALLOWS

pear and dried cherry cobbler

This is my favorite kind of dessert —practically foolproof, yet utterly irresistible. Here, a really easy crust tops fragrant, ripe pears and plump dried cherries perfect for fall. Pop this in the oven while you're fixing the rest of the meal. This is great on its own and outstanding with vanilla ice cream.

Preheat the oven to 375°F.

To make the filling: Peel, halve, and core the pears. Cut into $1/2$-inch-thick slices and transfer to a medium bowl. Add the sugar, cornstarch, ginger, and cinnamon and toss to mix. Gently fold in the cherries. Transfer to a 2-quart baking dish.

To make the topping: Put the flour, sugar, baking powder, salt, ginger, and cinnamon in the bowl of an electric mixer fitted with the paddle attachment and mix until well blended. Alternatively, mix this by hand in a bowl with a whisk.

Add the butter, piece by piece, and mix until the dough resembles cornmeal. If making by hand, use a pastry cutter or your fingers. Slowly add the milk, mixing in the mixer or with a wooden spoon, until the dough comes together and forms a ball. Turn out onto a lightly floured work surface and roll into a circle $1/4$ to $1/2$ inch thick.

Use the baking dish as a guide to cut the dough to the size of the top of the cobbler. There will not be much excess dough, if any. Carefully lift the dough from the work surface and lay it over the fruit.

Brush the dough with the cream and bake for about 50 minutes, or until golden brown and bubbling around the edges. Serve warm.

SERVES 6

FILLING

2 pounds ripe, firm pears (6 to 7 pears)

$1/2$ cup sugar

1 tablespoon cornstarch

$1/2$ teaspoon ground ginger

$1/2$ teaspoon ground cinnamon

$1/2$ cup dried cherries

TOPPING

1 cup all-purpose flour, plus more for dusting

3 tablespoons sugar

1 teaspoon baking powder

$1/4$ teaspoon salt

$1/8$ teaspoon ground ginger

$1/8$ teaspoon ground cinnamon

3 tablespoons cold unsalted butter, cut into pieces

$1/3$ cup plus 1 tablespoon milk

1 tablespoon heavy cream

Call the Kids

- Measure the sugar
- Toss the pears with the sugar, cornstarch, ginger, and cinnamon
- Add the cherries
- Measure the flour
- Mix the dough by hand
- Roll out the dough
- Brush the dough with cream

grandma's old-fashioned bread

My grandmother Stephanie taught me to bake this bread, and it is well worth the time it takes. It has a wonderfully chewy crust and a satisfying texture, and it is as good eaten by the slice as when it's used for sandwiches. Don't be put off by nine cups of flour. If you're going to take the time to bake bread, make several loaves. This freezes well and can be reheated.

2 cups milk

1 cup water plus $^1/_3$ cup warm water

1 cup sugar

6 tablespoons ($^3/_4$ stick) unsalted butter

$3^3/_4$ teaspoons active dry yeast (about 1$^1/_2$ packets)

9 cups all-purpose flour, plus more for dusting

6 whole allspice, crushed

$^1/_2$ cup golden raisins (optional)

2 teaspoons salt

4 large eggs, lightly beaten

Olive oil

EGG WASH

1 large egg

1 tablespoon milk

Call the Kids

- Measure the milk and water
- Measure the sugar
- Measure the flour
- Measure the raisins and salt
- Mix together the flour, allspice, raisins, and salt
- Knead the dough
- Punch down the dough
- Grease the bowl and baking pans
- Whisk the egg wash together

In a small saucepan, bring the milk and 1 cup of the water to a boil. Remove from the heat and stir in the sugar and butter until the sugar dissolves and the butter melts.

In a glass measuring cup, sprinkle the yeast over the remaining $^1/_3$ cup warm water and set aside to dissolve until foamy.

Put the flour in a large mixing bowl. Add the allspice, raisins, if using, and salt and whisk to mix well. Make a well in the center of the flour. Add the eggs, the yeast mixture, and the milk mixture. Stir with a large spoon until all the ingredients are incorporated and the dough is firm. If the dough is very sticky, add a little more flour.

Remove the dough from the bowl and knead on a lightly floured surface for 4 to 5 minutes or until smooth and elastic.

Lightly oil a bowl with olive oil. Transfer the dough to the bowl, cover with a clean kitchen towel, and allow to rise in a warm spot for 4 to 5 hours, or until doubled in bulk.

Lightly oil three 9 x 5 x 3-inch loaf pans or 2 baking sheets.

Punch the dough down in the bowl, turn out onto a lightly floured surface, and knead two or three times. Form the dough into 3 elongated loaves and divide among the pans. Alternatively, form into 3 free-standing round loaves and put them on the baking sheets. Cover the dough with clean kitchen towels and allow to rise for about 1 hour, or until nearly doubled in bulk.

Preheat the oven to 350°F.

Make the egg wash by whisking the egg and milk together in a small bowl. With a sharp knife, make crosshatch marks across the top of each loaf, about $^1/_4$ to $^1/_2$ inch deep and about 1 inch apart. Brush the tops of the loaves with the egg wash.

Bake for 55 to 60 minutes, or until the loaves are golden brown and sound "hollow" when tapped on the bottom. (If you're using loaf pans, unmold one loaf to check.) Turn the loaves out of the pans and let them cool on wire racks before slicing.

MAKES 3 LOAVES

indian pudding

When I was in school in Boston, I loved to eat at Durgin-Park, an old-time restaurant that serves traditional New England fare and is nothing if not a local institution. I quickly fell in love with Indian pudding, a rich, sweet mixture of molasses, cornmeal, butter, and eggs—an intoxicating combination for a cold winter day. It's really easy to make, and when you add a scoop of cold vanilla ice cream to the dessert, it's irresistible!

Preheat the oven to 300°F. Grease a glass 8 x 8 x 2-inch baking dish with butter.

In a heavy saucepan, combine the cornmeal and salt. Set the pan over medium heat and slowly add the milk, whisking to mix; bring to a boil. Reduce the heat to medium low and simmer for about 10 minutes, or until thick and creamy. Whisk in the butter and remove from the heat.

In a large mixing bowl, whisk together the eggs, molasses, brown sugar, and ginger. Gradually whisk this into the cornmeal, a little at a time. (Adding this too quickly will scramble the eggs.) Pour the pudding into the prepared dish.

Put the dish in a roasting pan and pour enough hot water into the pan to come halfway up the sides of the glass dish. Carefully transfer the roasting pan to the oven.

Bake for 1 hour and 30 minutes, or until the pudding is just set. Remove the pudding dish from the roasting pan and serve the pudding warm with vanilla ice cream.

SERVES 6

1 tablespoon unsalted butter, plus extra
   for greasing the pan
$1/4$ cup yellow cornmeal
$1/4$ teaspoon salt
$2^1/_2$ cups milk
2 large eggs
$1/2$ cup molasses
2 tablespoons packed dark brown sugar
$1^1/_2$ teaspoons ground ginger
Vanilla ice cream

Call the Kids

- Grease the pan
- Measure the cornmeal
- Measure the milk
- Measure the brown sugar
- Whisk the eggs with the molasses, sugar, and ginger
- Pour the water into the roasting pan

gray's cinnamon jelly doughnuts

Homemade doughnuts are really fun and truly delicious, and kids are thrilled to see how doughnuts are made. If you've never made doughnuts, give them a try. They are one of those things you should make at least once, and when you get going, you'll find they are not hard. I suggest eating these the day they are made, which usually isn't a problem for most families!

2 to 2^1/$_4$ cups bread flour, plus extra for dusting

1 teaspoon ground cinnamon

^{1}/$_2$ teaspoon salt

^{1}/$_2$ cup warm milk

1 tablespoon granulated sugar

1^1/$_4$ teaspoons active dry yeast

1 large egg, beaten

1^1/$_2$ tablespoons unsalted butter, melted

About 6 cups vegetable oil, plus extra for greasing the bowl

Confectioners' sugar

^{1}/$_2$ cup seedless jam, such as raspberry or strawberry

Call the Kids

- Measure the flour, cinnamon, and salt
- Measure the milk
- Mix the milk with the sugar and yeast
- Mix the dough
- Grease the bowl
- Knead the dough
- Punch down the dough
- Cut out the doughnuts
- Fill the cooled doughnuts with jam

In the bowl of a food processor fitted with the metal blade, combine 2 cups of the flour, the cinnamon, and the salt.

In a small bowl, mix the milk, granulated sugar, and yeast. Let sit for about 5 minutes, or until the mixture bubbles slightly.

Add the yeast mixture, egg, and butter to the flour and pulse until the dough begins to form into a ball. Add more flour if the dough is too sticky.

Lightly oil a large bowl.

Turn out the dough onto a lightly floured board and knead for about 5 minutes, or until smooth and elastic. Transfer the dough to the oiled bowl, cover with a clean, dry dish towel or plastic wrap, and set aside in a warm part of the kitchen for 1 to 2 hours, or until doubled in bulk.

Turn the dough onto a lightly floured board and punch down to expel the air in the dough. Using a rolling pin, roll the dough out into a rectangle about ^{1}/$_2$ inch thick. Using a round, floured biscuit or cookie cutter, or a glass, cut out 2- to 3-inch rounds. Transfer the rounds to a lightly floured baking sheet, taking care not to crowd them. Reroll the scraps to make additional doughnuts.

Cover the doughnuts with a clean dish towel and set aside in a warm part of the kitchen for 15 to 20 minutes, or until doubled in size.

Pour the vegetable oil into a large, heavy pot (to a depth of 3 inches). Heat over medium-high heat until a deep-frying thermometer registers 350°F. Working carefully, drop 1 or 2 doughnuts at a time into the hot oil and fry for about 1 minute on each side, or until golden brown. Use long-handled tongs to turn the doughnuts.

Remove the doughnuts from the oil with the tongs and drain on paper towels. Sprinkle with confectioners' sugar and let the doughnuts cool.

With the tip of a paring knife, cut a small slit into the side of each doughnut. Fill a pastry bag fitted with a large plain tip with jam and pipe about 2 teaspoons into each doughnut. Sprinkle with more confectioners' sugar, if desired.

MAKES 10 TO 12 DOUGHNUTS

NOTE: For a homemade pastry bag, fill a sturdy plastic bag with the jam, cut a small corner off the bottom of the bag, and squeeze the filling through the opening.

TIP Deep-frying is a legitimate and delicious cooking technique that few of us try at home. This is a shame because when done right, the food is crunchy and light. It's really not hard and, with common-sense precautions, it is safe. Here are a few tips for frying in hot oil.

- Use vegetable oils with high smoking points such as canola, soybean, corn, and peanut. Olive oil is not a good choice for deep-frying.
- Heat the oil in a deep, heavy pot and clip a deep-fat thermometer to the pot to gauge when the temperature is right.
- Another way to tell if the oil is hot (about 350°F. for the frying in this book and most frying needs) is to insert the long handle of a wooden spoon into the oil. If bubbles immediately gather around the handle, the oil is hot enough to fry. This is the method I use more often and it never lets me down.
- A third method for determining if the oil is hot is to drop a few bread crumbs into the oil. If they sizzle, the oil is hot enough.
- Wear heavy oven mitts that cover your wrists. Gently lower food into the hot oil with tongs or a slotted spoon. If you drop it, it could splash. Use the same implements to gently lift food from the oil.
- Never crowd the pan. Too much food will lower the oil's temperature. If the oil is not hot enough, the food absorbs the oil.
- Always, always let the oil regain its 350°F. temperature between batches of food.
- Drain fried food on a wire rack set over a baking sheet or a plate lined with a few paper towels.

summer picnics

golden gazpacho ✳ corn and black bean salad ✳ asian flank steak salad ✳ shrimp salad with avocado, celery, and red onion ✳ turtle brownies

We love picnics, whether we travel no farther than the backyard or venture all the way to the beach or park. The meal I've assembled here travels well in a good cooler and has flavors and textures to appeal to everyone. My kids love the steak salad, which you can make with flank steak you've grilled the night before and then serve cold or at room temperature; my husband and I are sold on the shrimp salad, too. No one can resist the brownies with their caramel topping. Once we settle down at a picnic table or on a lawn, I find the meal especially relaxing—partly because I cannot jump up and run to the kitchen for *anything*!

Thermoses are great for transporting soups and drinks. Another idea is to freeze lemonade or limeade in a portable plastic jug the night before so that it will be just right when you reach the picnic site. Pack salads in rigid plastic containers. If you take sandwiches, wrap them very well in plastic wrap or wax paper and pack them in plastic containers with tight-fitting lids so that they don't get squashed. Finally, don't forget to take along plenty of napkins, drinking cups, enough utensils, a small cutting board, a bread knife (if you pack bread and cheese), and plastic trash bags. And, oh yes, the corkscrew!

golden gazpacho

Kids think it's cool that you can liquefy a bunch of raw ingredients and make soup—no cooking required! I've made this with yellow tomatoes, but if the red ones in your garden or at the local farm-stand look better, use them. You can cut back on the onions and add more peppers, for example, to suit your family's taste.

In the bowl of a food processor fitted with the metal blade or in a blender, pulse half of the tomatoes until they are still slightly chunky, then transfer to a large bowl. Purée the remaining tomatoes until smooth and add to the bowl.

Put the onion, bell pepper, cucumber, garlic, and jalapeño into the food processor and pulse until the vegetables are fairly smooth but still have a little texture. (Alternatively, the ingredients can be finely chopped by hand.) Add to the bowl with the tomatoes.

Stir in the tomato juice, olive oil, balsamic, and salt. Season to taste with pepper. If the gazpacho seems thick, stir in up to 1 cup water to loosen it. Refrigerate for at least 2 hours, or until well chilled. Garnish with basil leaves and serve.

SERVES 6 TO 8

2 pounds ripe yellow tomatoes (5 to 6 tomatoes), cored and cut into medium chunks
1 small white onion, coarsely chopped
1 large yellow bell pepper, seeded, ribs removed, coarsely chopped
1 large cucumber, peeled and coarsely chopped
2 garlic cloves, sliced
$1/2$ jalapeño pepper, seeded and diced
1 cup tomato juice
$1/4$ cup extra-virgin olive oil
1 tablespoon balsamic vinegar
1 tablespoon salt
Freshly ground pepper
About 12 fresh basil leaves, torn into pieces

Call the Kids
- Peel the cucumber with a hand-held peeler
- Measure the tomato juice
- Measure the oil
- Stir the soup ingredients together
- Pick and tear the basil leaves

USE YOUR JUDGMENT
- Pulse and purée the tomatoes in the food processor
- Pulse the vegetables in the food processor

corn and black bean salad

In the summer when sweet corn reigns supreme, most of us eat it straight off the cob. Nothing wrong with that! But, for this salad, I cut the kernels off the cob before cooking them; it takes minutes and they taste so fresh you'll be glad you took the extra step. The same for the black beans. Since I don't find it necessary to soak dried beans before cooking them, this is pretty easy. Mix these two with a lively vinaigrette made from lime juice and you end up with a vibrant summer salad shimmering with bright flavors and just a little heat.

$1/4$ cup plus 2 tablespoons olive oil (see Note)

1 teaspoon red pepper flakes

4 ounces ($1/2$ cup) dried black beans

12 ounces corn kernels (from 4 ears fresh corn; see page 161) or 12 ounces frozen corn

Juice of 1 lime

1 teaspoon salt

5 scallions, trimmed and thinly sliced, white and green parts

1 tablespoon chopped fresh cilantro (optional)

Call the Kids

- Measure the oil
- Measure the beans
- Cover the beans with water
- Squeeze the lime
- Whisk the vinaigrette ingredients
- Toss the salad

In a small saucepan, combine the olive oil with the red pepper flakes and heat gently over low heat. When very warm, remove from the heat and set aside to cool. You can make this up to 24 hours ahead of time.

In a small pot, cover the black beans with plenty of water and bring to a boil over high heat. Reduce the heat to medium and simmer for about 40 minutes, or until tender. Drain and set aside to cool.

In a saucepan, combine the corn kernels with enough cold water to cover. Bring to a boil over medium-high heat, reduce the heat to medium, and simmer for 3 to 4 minutes, or until the corn is tender. Drain and set aside to cool.

In a small bowl, whisk the lime juice with the salt until the salt is dissolved. Whisk in the chili oil.

In a bowl, toss together the beans, corn, and scallions. Add enough of the lime–chili vinaigrette to coat the salad and toss gently. Add the cilantro, if using. This can be made up to 1 day ahead and refrigerated.

SERVES 4 TO 6

NOTE: You can skip the step of the olive oil and red pepper flake infusion by substituting store-bought chili oil.

asian flank steak salad

Even if you don't make the salad, this is a great way to marinate and grill flank steak. You can grill the steak early in the day, when it's cool, and then refrigerate it until needed. You can assemble and toss the salad four to five hours in advance. It travels well, packed in a plastic container kept in a cooler. Kids love the Asian flavors, especially the peanut sauce.

Stir together the soy sauce, lime juice, scallions, garlic, and ginger in a shallow glass or ceramic dish. Add the flank steak, turning to coat both sides with the marinade. Cover and refrigerate for at least 6 hours and up to 12 hours.

Prepare a charcoal or gas grill so that the coals or heating elements are medium hot. Off the heat, lightly spray the grate with vegetable oil spray.

Lift the steak from the marinade and scrape off as much of the marinade as you can. Season the steak with salt and pepper and grill for 5 to 6 minutes on each side for medium rare. Allow the steak to rest about 5 minutes and then cut against the grain on the bias into $1/4$-inch-thick slices. Set aside.

In a large bowl, combine the greens, cabbages, bell pepper, carrots, bean sprouts, and sesame seeds. Add the peanut sauce, season with salt and pepper, and toss to combine. Add the flank steak and toss to combine; serve. You can make this up to 4 or 5 hours before serving.

SERVES 4

1 cup soy sauce
Juice of 2 limes
4 scallions, roots removed, thinly sliced
3 garlic cloves, thinly sliced
One 3-inch piece fresh ginger, peeled and thinly sliced
1 pound flank steak
Flavorless vegetable oil spray
Salt and freshly ground pepper
1 cup Asian salad greens, mesclun greens, or other young, tender greens
1 cup shredded napa cabbage
1 cup shredded red cabbage
1 red bell pepper, seeded and thinly sliced
2 small carrots, peeled and shredded
1 cup bean sprouts
1 tablespoon sesame seeds
$1/2$ cup Peanut Dipping Sauce (page 118)

Call the Kids

- Measure the soy sauce
- Squeeze the limes
- Turn the steak in the marinade
- Measure the greens and sprouts
- Peel the carrots
- Toss the salad
- Add the peanut sauce and toss again

USE YOUR JUDGMENT

- Shred the cabbage

shrimp salad with avocado, celery, and red onion

This shrimp salad is a wonderful lunch or picnic dish because it's so easy and yet always special. The lemon vinaigrette is a refreshing change from the mayonnaise that dresses many similar salads. I suggest you give yourself a break and buy the shrimp already cooked. Buy the freshest and the best shrimp you can.

1/4 cup extra-virgin olive oil

1 tablespoon plus 2 teaspoons fresh lemon juice

Salt and freshly ground pepper

24 large, cooked peeled shrimp (about 1 pound)

1 ripe avocado, pitted, peeled, and diced

1 celery rib, thinly sliced

1 scallion, white and green parts, sliced

12 grape tomatoes, halved

1 1/2 tablespoons chopped fresh flat-leaf parsley leaves

1 tablespoon diced red onion

In a small bowl, whisk together all the olive oil and lemon juice and season with salt and pepper. Set aside until needed. Whisk just before using.

In a large bowl, combine the shrimp, avocado, celery, scallion, tomatoes, parsley, and red onion. Sprinkle with enough vinaigrette to coat lightly. Toss the shrimp salad gently and season to taste with salt and pepper.

SERVES 4

Call the Kids

- Measure the oil
- Squeeze the lemon
- Dice the avocado with a blunt knife
- Mix the ingredients for the vinaigrette
- Mix the ingredients for the salad
- Toss the shrimp with the vinaigrette

turtle brownies

The base batter for these brownies is my favorite, the one I have made for years. Because I stir melted chocolate into the batter and then fold in whole chocolate chips just before baking, the brownies are deep, dark, and fudgy and especially moist with little pockets of extra melty chocolate. If your kids don't like the nutty topping, leave it off; the brownies are pretty great on their own. For a picnic, pack these in a single layer in a shallow plastic container with a tight-fitting lid.

Preheat the oven to 350°F. Grease a 13 x 9 x 2-inch baking dish with butter.

In a large saucepan, melt the butter over medium heat. Add the sugar and water and bring to a boil over medium-high heat.

Remove from the heat and add half of the chocolate chips. Stir until smooth.

Whisk in the eggs one at a time, making sure each is incorporated before adding the next.

In a separate bowl, whisk together the flour, salt, and baking soda. Gently mix into the chocolate mixture and when blended, stir in the remaining chocolate chips and the vanilla.

Pour the batter into the baking dish and bake for 30 to 35 minutes, or until the center of the brownies feels just firm. Cool on a wire rack.

Meanwhile, make the topping. In a heavy saucepan, bring the sugar, corn syrup, water, and the salt to a boil over medium heat and stir until the sugar dissolves. Stop stirring and let the caramel cook until it turns golden, 10 to 15 minutes.

Remove the pan from the heat and carefully add the cream and vanilla. The hot caramel may spatter when you add the cream, so wear oven mitts and stand back. This is not a task for kids.

When the caramel stops bubbling excessively, stir until smooth, and then stir in the pecans.

Spread the topping over the cooled brownies in an even layer. Let cool, and then cut the brownies into 16 squares.

MAKES 16 BROWNIES

BROWNIES

10 tablespoons (1^{1}/$_{4}$ sticks) unsalted butter, plus extra for greasing the baking dish

1^{1}/$_{2}$ cups sugar

^{1}/$_{4}$ cup water

24 ounces semisweet chocolate chips

5 large eggs

1^{1}/$_{2}$ cups all-purpose flour

^{1}/$_{2}$ teaspoon salt

^{1}/$_{2}$ teaspoon baking soda

1 teaspoon pure vanilla extract

CARAMEL PECAN TOPPING

1^{1}/$_{2}$ cups sugar

^{2}/$_{3}$ cup light corn syrup

6 tablespoons water

Pinch of salt

^{2}/$_{3}$ cup heavy cream

2 teaspoons pure vanilla extract

3 cups pecan halves or pieces

Call the Kids

- Grease the baking dish
- Measure the sugar and water
- Add the eggs to the batter
- Measure the flour
- Whisk together the flour, salt, and baking soda
- Stir the batter
- Measure the topping ingredients

afternoon snacks

Kids seem to be most hungry when they get home from school—and they want something fast! After they've thrown their backpacks on the floor, they inevitably ask, "What's there to eat?" You may prefer they eat something savory and filling, such as a quesadilla, or you may offer them something sweet and indulgent, such as a square of snack cake or slice of banana bread. The choice may depend on how close it is to dinnertime or, more realistically, on what you have in the house. The strawberry soup and yogurt parfait are easy to whip up, while you may have prepared the cake earlier in the day or week. You can go beyond what we suggest here with more elaborate sandwiches or different fillings for the quesadillas, or simplify with easy snacks such as apples, peanut butter, and graham crackers.

yogurt, granola, and berry parfait

This parfait is great as a snack, but we also like it for breakfast. It is sort of like a healthful sundae. We make it in a parfait glass, but any clear glass works well and once they start to layer the ingredients, kids quickly figure out others they can add or substitute, such as sliced peaches or bananas, raisins, and other flavors of yogurt. You can make these with your favorite store-bought granola or with the recipe on page 27.

Put half of the yogurt in a parfait glass or similar bowl. Sprinkle with half of the granola, and then top with the berries. Top with the remaining yogurt and granola. Garnish with a few berries.

SERVES 1

^{1}/$_2$ cup vanilla yogurt

^{1}/$_4$ cup granola

^{1}/$_3$ cup fresh berries, such as strawberries, blueberries, or raspberries (if using strawberries, hull and halve them), plus a few extra for garnishing

Call the Kids
- Measure the yogurt
- Measure the granola
- Layer the ingredients in the parfait glass

ham, cheddar, and tomato quesadillas

A ham-and-cheese quesadilla is a tempting alternative to a more standard sandwich, and it's just as easy and quick to make. Kids go crazy for crunchy, cheesy, melty quesadillas, and I have to confess a special fondness for them, too. I buy at least three packages of tortillas every time I shop and keep the extras in the freezer. That's how fast we go through them in our family!

Four 6-inch flour tortillas

1 cup shredded Cheddar cheese

3 ounces thinly sliced ham

1 ripe tomato, cored and thinly sliced

2 teaspoons unsalted butter

Call the Kids

- Measure the cheese
- Spread the cheese on the tortillas
- Put the ham and tomatoes on top of the cheese

On a flat surface, lay out 2 of the tortillas. Evenly spread the cheese over the tortillas, nearly to the edge. Top with ham and tomato slices. Put the remaining tortillas on top to make 2 quesadillas.

In a small sauté pan, melt 1 teaspoon of the butter over medium heat until bubbly. Put a quesadilla in the pan and cook for 2 to 3 minutes on each side, or until golden brown and the cheese melts. Remove the cooked quesadilla and set aside.

Melt the remaining teaspoon of butter and cook the second quesadilla. Slice each quesadilla into 8 wedges and serve immediately.

SERVES 2

chilled peach and strawberry soup

If I take this to the beach in a big thermos, my kids are happy. It tides them over between lunch and dinner, or can even be served as part of lunch. Beyond this, it's so simple to make and so refreshing, it can be a breakfast treat or a dessert, served with a scoop of sorbet.

In a heavy saucepan, combine the peaches, cranberry juice, peach nectar, water, strawberries, lime zest and juice, honey, and cinnamon stick and bring to a boil over medium-high heat. Reduce the heat and simmer for 30 minutes, or until the peaches are soft and mushy.

Remove from the heat. Working in batches, purée the soup in a blender until smooth. Set aside to cool. Cover and chill for at least 4 hours before serving.

SERVES 8 TO 10

$2^1/_2$ to 3 pounds ripe peaches
(about 6 peaches), pitted and cut
into large dice
$2^1/_2$ cups cranberry juice
2 cups peach nectar
1 cup water
8 large strawberries, hulled and halved
Zest and juice of 1 lime
2 tablespoons honey
1 cinnamon stick

Call the Kids

- Dice the peaches with a blunt knife
- Measure the cranberry juice, peach nectar, and water
- Hull and halve the strawberries with a blunt knife

USE YOUR JUDGMENT

- Purée the soup

banana nut bread

This is similar to one of the first bread recipes I mastered when I was a kid. It still ranks high on my list as nearly instant gratification: easy to mix and ready in an hour. My kids love mashing the bananas and then eating the baked bread. Although the recipe says to let the bread cool completely before slicing, this hardly ever happens in our house.

Unsalted butter

$^1/_2$ cup canola oil

1 cup sugar

2 cups mashed bananas, about 3 ripe bananas

2 large eggs, beaten

2 cups all-purpose flour

1 teaspoon baking soda

$^1/_2$ teaspoon baking powder

$^1/_2$ teaspoon salt

$^1/_2$ cup finely chopped walnuts (optional)

3 tablespoons milk

1 teaspoon pure vanilla extract

Preheat the oven to 350°F. Grease a 9 x 5 x 3-inch loaf pan with butter.

In a large bowl and using a wire whisk, whisk together the oil and sugar until blended. Add the bananas and eggs and mix well with a wooden spoon.

In a large bowl, combine the flour, baking soda, baking powder, and salt. Whisk well with a wire whisk. Gradually add to the banana mixture and stir until incorporated. Do not overmix. There will be some streaks of flour, which is fine.

Stir in the nuts, milk, and vanilla and mix until evenly distributed.

Pour and scrape the batter into the loaf pan. Bake for 60 to 70 minutes, or until a toothpick inserted in the center comes out clean.

Invert the loaf and remove it from the pan. Let the loaf cool right side up on a wire rack.

MAKES ONE 9-INCH LOAF

Call the Kids
- Grease the loaf pan
- Measure the oil and sugar
- Mash the bananas
- Measure the flour
- Whisk the ingredients together
- Measure the nuts
- Pour the batter into the loaf pan

easy snack cake

This pleasing butter cake is a good one to have waiting for your kids when they come home from school. It's one of those cakes you cut right in the pan and then keep in the pan covered with foil or a clean dish towel for easy access later on (and if your house is like mine, there will be a kitchen knife in the pan to cut the squares). The dusting of confectioners' sugar is all this cake needs, although you could choose to frost the top of the sheet cake with the Vanilla Frosting on page 171 or the Homestyle Chocolate Frosting on page 187. And although it may sound like a cliché, a glass of ice-cold milk is the ideal partner for this cake!

Preheat the oven to 350°F. Spray a 13 x 9 x 2-inch baking pan with vegetable oil spray, or butter it.

In a medium bowl, whisk together the flour, baking powder, and salt. In the bowl of an electric mixer fitted with the paddle attachment, beat the butter on medium speed for 1 to 2 minutes, or until smooth and light. Add the granulated sugar, $1/4$ cup at a time, scraping the sides of the bowl several times during mixing. Add the eggs one at a time and beat well after each addition. Add the vanilla and mix.

Reduce the speed to low and add the dry ingredients alternating with the milk, beginning and ending with the flour mixture. Beat for about 1 minute longer, or until the batter is smooth.

Pour the batter into the prepared pan and bake for 40 to 45 minutes, or until a toothpick inserted in the center comes out dry or until the cake is slightly springy to the touch. Put the cake pan on a wire cooling rack to cool.

Let the cake cool completely before dusting with confectioners' sugar. Cut into squares for serving directly from the pan.

MAKES ONE 13 X 9-INCH SHEET CAKE

Flavorless vegetable oil spray
3 cups sifted cake flour
1 tablespoon baking powder
$1/4$ teaspoon salt
1 cup (2 sticks) unsalted butter, softened
$1^3/4$ cups granulated sugar
4 large eggs, at room temperature
$1^1/2$ teaspoons pure vanilla extract
1 cup milk
Confectioners' sugar

Call the Kids

- Grease the pan
- Measure and whisk the flour, baking powder, and salt
- Beat the butter and sugar
- Add the eggs to the batter
- Add the dry ingredients and milk to the batter
- Fill the cake pan
- Dust the cake with confectioners' sugar

lazy winter weekends

chicken pot pie with cornmeal crust ❋ arugula and prosciutto pizza ❋ butternut squash gnocchi ❋ wild mushroom risotto ❋ white chicken chili

Days when you know a storm is coming or the forecast is for dreary, damp weather are custom-made for dishes that take some tending, some waiting, and then maybe a little more attention later on. Keeping tabs on the food is part of the pleasure of cooking and as an added benefit, the house is filled all day with delicious aromas. For example, while the butternut squash is roasting and then cooling for the gnocchi, or when the gnocchi dough is chilling, you can join in the Monopoly game in progress in front of the living-room fire. Enjoying the process is a big part of making these dishes, and while no one would make them all on the same weekend, we usually make more food than we can eat so that we can call the neighbors to join us for supper. I can't think of a better way to spend a lazy winter weekend!

chicken pot pie with cornmeal crust

Since I was a kid, I have had a soft spot for chicken pot pies. I grew up eating frozen pot pies, which I always liked, but when I learned to cook I knew I could do better. After a number of tries, I came up with this recipe, which has the classic creamy chicken filling and a not-so-classic, crunchy cornmeal crust. It's a great one-dish meal for the family or for casual entertaining, served with a big green salad.

Preheat the oven to 400°F.

To make the filling for the pot pie: If using fresh pearl onions, fill a small saucepan with water and bring to a boil over medium-high heat. Add the pearl onions and blanch for about 3 minutes. Drain and set aside to cool. Peel the onions using a small paring knife and set aside.

In a large saucepan, melt the butter over medium heat. Add the carrots, celery, and onion and slowly cook the vegetables for about 10 minutes, stirring occasionally, without letting them color. Add the flour to the pan and cook, stirring frequently, for 5 to 6 minutes. Add the chicken stock, slowly at first, stirring vigorously to incorporate it with the vegetables.

Add the potatoes and chicken, bring to a simmer, and cook for about 10 minutes, or until the potatoes are tender. Add the peas and pearl onions and cook for another minute or so to heat through. Season with the salt and with pepper to taste. Transfer to a 13 x 9 x 2-inch baking dish.

To make the topping: Put the butter, cornmeal, flour, sugar, baking powder, salt, and eggs in the bowl of a food processor fitted with a metal blade. Pulse until just combined but still crumbly.

Add the milk and pulse just until incorporated. Pour the batter over the chicken filling to cover completely. Bake for about 40 minutes, or until the crust turns golden and the filling is bubbling around the edges.

SERVES 10 TO 12

NOTE: To make this ahead of time, prepare the chicken mixture and top it with crust ahead of time and refrigerate for up to 1 day. Bake for the same length of time and check the pot pie. It might need 5 or 10 minutes longer if it was very cold when you put it in the oven.

FILLING

1 pound pearl onions or frozen, peeled pearl onions

3/4 cup (1 1/2 sticks) unsalted butter

2 large carrots, peeled and cut into small dice

3 celery ribs, cut into small dice

1 medium onion, cut into small dice

3/4 cup all-purpose flour

6 cups chicken stock or low-sodium broth

2 potatoes, peeled and cut into small dice

2 cups shredded, cooked chicken breast

1 cup frozen or fresh shelled peas

1 tablespoon plus 1 teaspoon salt

Freshly ground pepper

CORNMEAL TOPPING

1/2 cup (1 stick) unsalted butter

1 1/2 cups cornmeal

1 1/2 cups all-purpose flour

1/3 cup sugar

4 teaspoons baking powder

1 1/2 teaspoons salt

2 large eggs

1 1/2 cups milk

Call the Kids

- Peel the carrots
- Measure the flour and stock
- Measure the cornmeal, flour, sugar, and milk

arugula and prosciutto pizza

Kids love the fun of making pizza at home—plus it always tastes better than delivery pizza. Admittedly the topping is a little more sophisticated than some, but adults and older kids will appreciate it. For younger children, make a simple cheese pizza. But the real star of the recipe is the pizza dough, which is the best I have ever tasted. I first saw the recipe in a book by food writer Patricia Wells and was inspired to make one nearly like it. I never looked elsewhere. I try to make the dough the night before or first thing in the morning and let it sit in the refrigerator all day. It's then ready to be punched down and rolled into pizzas—a forgiving and completely reliable dough.

Preheat the oven to 400°F.

Punch down the pizza dough and turn it out onto a floured surface. Divide into 2 pieces. Stretch each piece of dough into a circle that is roughly 10 to 12 inches in diameter and $1/4$ inch thick. Transfer each circle of the pizza dough to a baking sheet or pizza stone.

Spoon half of the marinara sauce over each crust. Spread it to cover, leaving about $1/2$ inch around the edges. Arrange the mozzarella evenly on top of the sauce.

Bake each pizza for 15 to 18 minutes, or until the cheese starts to bubble and the crust turns golden brown.

Meanwhile, in a small bowl, toss the arugula with the olive oil and the vinegar and season with salt and pepper.

Remove the pizzas from the oven and sprinkle the prosciutto over the top. Distribute the arugula evenly over the pizzas. Cut each pizza into 4 slices and serve immediately.

SERVES 4; MAKES TWO 10- TO 12-INCH PIZZAS

Pizza dough (page 94)

$1^1/3$ cups Aux Délices's Marinara Sauce (page 129), or your favorite store-bought tomato sauce

8 ounces fresh mozzarella, thinly sliced

2 large handfuls baby arugula

2 tablespoons extra-virgin olive oil

1 tablespoon balsamic vinegar

Salt and freshly ground pepper

4 ounces thinly sliced prosciutto

Call the Kids

- Measure the water
- Mix the water, sugar, and yeast
- Add the olive oil and salt
- Measure and add the flour
- Oil the bowl
- Knead the dough
- Punch down the dough
- Stretch the dough into a circle
- Measure the sauce
- Spread the sauce over the dough
- Lay the cheese on the pizza
- Toss the arugula with the oil and vinegar
- Top the pizza with prosciutto and arugula

butternut squash gnocchi

These are a nice, light change from potato gnocchi, and the flavor of the squash goes sublimely with sage and butter (two flavors I also love with sweet potato). Kids love rolling the ropes of dough and cutting them into little pillows of dough, which makes them much easier to form than classic gnocchi, which are rolled off a fork to create small ridges. Serve these all on their own as a main course or try them as a first course or alongside simply cooked chicken, lamb, or fish. The pleasing soft texture and warm flavors of the gnocchi leave you feeling comforted and entirely content.

GNOCCHI

1 medium butternut squash, about
   2 pounds
1/4 cup olive oil
Salt and freshly ground pepper
3/4 cup whole-milk ricotta cheese
3/4 cup freshly grated Parmesan cheese
1 large egg
1 1/3 to 1 2/3 cups all-purpose flour, plus
   more for dusting

SAUCE

1/2 cup (1 stick) unsalted butter
1 small bunch sage, leaves picked and
   chopped
1/2 cup freshly grated Parmesan cheese
Salt and freshly ground pepper

Call the Kids

- Scrape the seeds from the squash
- Mash the roasted squash
- Measure the cheeses
- Mix together the cheeses, egg, and squash
- Add the flour to make a dough
- Divide the dough into 4 pieces
- Roll the dough into ropes and cut into pieces with a blunt knife

Preheat the oven to 350°F.

Slice the ends off the butternut squash and cut in half crosswise where the bulb starts. Peel using a vegetable peeler. Cut the bulb-shaped end in half and scoop out the seeds with a spoon; discard. Cut the squash into 1-inch pieces.

Transfer the squash to a baking pan, drizzle with the olive oil, and season with salt and pepper. Roast, uncovered, for 45 to 55 minutes, or until softened.

Mash the roasted squash with a fork or potato masher or process it until smooth in a food processor fitted with the metal blade. Transfer to a large bowl and set aside to cool for 10 to 15 minutes.

Stir the ricotta, Parmesan, and egg into the squash. Add 2 teaspoons of salt and 1 1/3 cups of the flour. Stir well with a wooden spoon until the mixture forms a soft dough, adding more flour if needed.

Transfer the squash dough to a lightly floured work surface and work the dough lightly to form it into a ball. If it is sticky, add a little more flour. Transfer to a bowl, cover with a clean dish towel, and refrigerate for at least 2 hours.

Divide the dough into 4 balls. Using your palms, roll each ball on a flat surface dusted with flour into a long rope about 1/2 inch in diameter. Cut these into 1/2- to 3/4-inch-long pieces, or gnocchi.

Bring a large pot of water to a boil and add 1 tablespoon salt. Drop the gnocchi into the boiling water. Let the water return to the boil and when the gnocchi bob to the surface, cook for about 2 minutes. To check for doneness, remove one and cut it in half to see if it's cooked through.

Lift the gnocchi out with a slotted spoon, drain well, and transfer to a serving bowl.

To make the sauce, in a saucepan large enough to hold the gnocchi, melt the butter with the sage over medium-low heat. When the butter begins to bubble, add the gnocchi and cook until heated through and the butter and sage are golden brown. Sprinkle with the Parmesan cheese, season with salt and pepper, toss, and serve.

SERVES 4 AS A MAIN COURSE; 8 AS A SIDE DISH

wild mushroom risotto

Kids love the creamy, full flavor of risotto, preferring it to plain steamed rice. Once they learn the technique for making it, which requires some patience, they will immediately see how they can add something other than mushrooms, if they so desire (see Note below). You can make this with any of the assortment of fresh mushrooms on display in most supermarkets, or with the more ordinary white button mushrooms. Either way, this is a winner!

Approximately 7$^{1}/_{2}$ cups chicken stock
  or low-sodium broth
6 tablespoons ($^{3}/_{4}$ stick) unsalted butter
6 shallots, finely chopped
2 cups Arborio rice
1 cup white wine
1 pound assorted mushrooms, such as
  shiitake and cremini, or plain white
  button mushrooms, cleaned and
  sliced
3 tablespoons mascarpone cheese
1 tablespoon salt, or to taste
Freshly ground pepper
Chopped fresh flat-leaf parsley or
  snipped fresh chives
Freshly grated Parmesan cheese
  (optional)

Call the Kids
- Measure the stock
- Measure the rice
  USE YOUR JUDGMENT
- Add the stock to the risotto
- Stir the risotto
- Stir in the cheese, salt, and pepper

In a large saucepan, heat the chicken stock over medium-high heat until hot. Reduce the heat just so the stock stays hot but is not bubbling.

In a heavy saucepan, melt the butter over medium heat until just bubbling. Add the shallots and sauté for 4 to 5 minutes, or until they are softened and lightly colored. Turn up the heat to medium high and add the rice. Sauté, stirring with a long-handled wooden spoon, for 1 minute, and then add the white wine and mushrooms. Stir until the wine evaporates completely.

Begin to add the hot chicken stock, $^{1}/_{2}$ cup at a time, using a long-handled ladle. After each addition, stir the rice gently until the stock has been absorbed before adding more. The risotto should simmer gently while you add the stock to it. It will take 18 to 20 minutes to add all the stock. After this time, the rice should still have a little bite, but not be too hard, and it should still be soupy, not dry. If it is not al dente, add some additional hot stock or water until the rice is soft.

When the risotto is done, turn off the heat. Stir in the mascarpone cheese. Add the salt and pepper, taste, and adjust the seasoning if necessary. Garnish with parsley and sprinkle with Parmesan cheese, if using.

SERVES·4

NOTE: Depending on your family's preferences, any number of ingredients can be added by the handful near the end of cooking, once the rice is cooked: Cooked fresh or frozen peas, blanched asparagus (see page 147), grilled vegetables, strips of prosciutto, diced artichoke hearts, and diced cooked shrimp or lobster meat are some of our favorites.

white chicken chili

As I am sure is true of many families, chicken is a staple in our house and so I am always on the look-out for new ways to serve it. Chicken chili has lighter flavors than beef chili and the kids love it. This recipe takes a little time, although I don't soak the beans before cooking them (there's no need to), but it's not difficult and is well worth the wait.

In a large saucepan, bring the chicken pieces and stock to a simmer over medium-high heat. Lower the heat to medium and poach the chicken, skimming off any fat that accumulates on the surface, for 18 to 20 minutes, or until just done. Remove the chicken from the stock and set aside until cool enough to handle. Reserve the stock in the pan.

Remove and discard the skin and bones from the chicken. Shred the chicken meat, set aside on a plate or in a shallow bowl, cover, and refrigerate until needed.

In a large sauté pan, heat the oil over medium-high heat until shimmering. Add the onions, celery, garlic, and jalapeños, if using, and sauté, stirring occasionally, for 8 to 10 minutes, until softened but not colored. Remove from the heat and set aside.

In the saucepan holding the reserved poaching liquid, mix together the white beans, cumin, and cinnamon stick. Bring to a simmer over medium heat and simmer for about 1½ hours, or until the beans are tender but not mushy. Remove and discard the cinnamon stick.

Stir in the shredded chicken and the sautéed vegetables and season with salt and pepper.

Just before serving, stir in the cheese, parsley, and cilantro.

SERVES 6 TO 8

4 bone-in chicken breasts
  (about 3 pounds)
8 cups chicken stock or low-sodium
  broth
3 tablespoons extra-virgin olive oil
2 small onions, chopped
2 celery ribs, diced
4 garlic cloves, sliced
2 medium jalapeño peppers, seeded
  and finely chopped (optional)
1 pound dried white beans, such as
  Great Northern
1 tablespoon plus 1 teaspoon ground
  cumin
1-inch cinnamon stick
Salt and freshly ground pepper
2 cups grated white Cheddar cheese
1/4 cup chopped fresh flat-leaf parsley
  leaves
1/4 cup chopped fresh cilantro leaves

Call the Kids
- Measure the stock
- Shred the cooled cooked chicken
- Mix the beans and spices in the saucepan
- Tear the leaves off the herbs

kids' parties

my favorite salad ✳ individual cheese pizzas ✳ tropical

chicken skewers with mango yogurt dipping sauce ✳

raspberry-filled sugar cookie hearts ✳ flowerpot cakes

We give a lot of kids' parties at Aux Délices and it's always great fun. These are cooking parties that involve hands-on experiences for the kids, as well as ample time for good eating. A cooking party can be as simple as a play date or a little more festive for a birthday. In this chapter, I have recipes that are fun for kids to make and to eat. The individual pizzas are always a hit; kids like to assemble and then devour the chicken skewers; and they really get into decorating the flowerpot cakes with gummy worms—and then digging straight into the pots with gleeful gluttony!

An at-home party might not include all the dishes in this chapter; you might decide that the pizza and the cake are more than enough, or the salad, chicken, and cookies work just fine. Much depends on the number and age of the children, your organizational skills, and if you're on your own or have enlisted the help of other adults. Arrange the ingredients, bowls, and utensils ahead of time. Encourage the kids to clean up after making one dish before moving on to the next.

To make the party easier to orchestrate, you may elect to wash the greens for the salad or cut the chicken and mango before the party begins and keep them in containers in the refrigerator. Or, make the pizza dough beforehand and then let the kids roll it out and put the toppings on it. After they've eaten, you could teach them how to make the dough from scratch and then pack lumps of dough in plastic bags for them to take home, where it can be prepared or frozen for later use. The same strategy works for the Raspberry-Filled Sugar Cookie Hearts: You make the dough and the kids will be happy rolling it out and forming the cookies.

my favorite salad

Several years ago, I started adding healthful dried fruits and nuts to the usual mix of fresh greens, and ever since, this salad has been my favorite. I can't get enough of the crunchiness and sweetness they bring. For the next kids' party, encourage kids to add as much or as little as they like of all kinds of good things such as raisins, apples, and cherry tomatoes—or different fruits and vegetables to make their favorite salads. You don't have to make it exactly as I suggest, but this provides a good starting point for creating your own tossed salad.

In a large bowl, combine the salad greens, apple, raisins, almonds, tomatoes, scallions, carrots, and avocado for the salad.

To mix the vinaigrette, in a small bowl, combine the vinegar, shallot, and 1 teaspoon salt. Whisk until the salt is dissolved. Slowly add the olive oil and whisk until incorporated. Season with pepper and more salt, if necessary.

Toss the salad with just enough vinaigrette to wet lightly. Season with salt and pepper and serve.

SERVES 4 TO 6

SALAD

4 cups mixed salad greens such as
    mesclun, Boston lettuce, or red leaf
    lettuce, washed and dried
1 apple or pear, peeled, cored, and
    sliced
$1/3$ cup raisins or dried cranberries
$1/2$ cup slivered or whole almonds
12 grape or cherry tomatoes, halved
2 scallions, white and green parts,
    sliced on the bias
2 carrots, peeled and grated
1 avocado, pitted, peeled, and diced

BALSAMIC VINAIGRETTE

$1/3$ cup balsamic vinegar
1 shallot, finely diced
Salt and freshly ground pepper
$2/3$ cup extra-virgin olive oil

Call the Kids
- Wash and dry the lettuce
- Peel the apple and carrots with a
  hand-held peeler
- Measure the raisins and almonds
- Dice the avocado with a blunt knife
- Measure the vinegar and oil
- Whisk the vinaigrette
- Toss the salad

individual cheese pizzas

These are great because everyone rolls out his own round of dough and tops it with as much sauce and cheese as he likes. Every pizza comes out a little differently, but that's the fun of it! This is great pizza dough, very easy to put together. I prefer bread flour because it produces a tender crust, but all-purpose is fine. When I make the dough, I usually double the recipe and freeze half.

PIZZA DOUGH

$1^1/_3$ cups warm water

$1^1/_2$ teaspoons sugar

1 teaspoon active dry yeast

$2^1/_2$ tablespoons olive oil, plus more for greasing the bowl

$1^1/_4$ teaspoons salt

1 pound ($3^3/_4$ cups) bread flour, plus extra for rolling

PIZZA TOPPING

$1^1/_2$ cups Aux Délices's Marinara Sauce (page 129), or store-bought tomato sauce

2 cups shredded mozzarella cheese

Call the Kids

- Measure the water
- Mix the ingredients for the dough
- Knead the dough
- Grease the bowl
- Punch down the dough
- Form the dough into individual pizzas
- Measure the sauce
- Spread the sauce over the dough
- Measure the cheese
- Put the cheese on the pizza

In a large bowl, combine the water, sugar, and yeast and let stand for 5 or 6 minutes, or until it bubbles slightly. Stir in the olive oil and salt.

Add the flour, bit by bit, stirring with a wooden spoon until most of the flour has been absorbed and the dough forms a ball. Turn the dough onto a floured surface and knead for about 5 minutes, or until the dough is soft and smooth. Form into a ball with your hands.

Generously rub the inside of a large bowl with olive oil and put the dough in the bowl. Turn the dough over so that all sides are lightly coated with the oil. Cover the bowl with plastic wrap or a clean dish towel and refrigerate overnight. This dough needs at least 10 hours to rise and can be refrigerated for 24 hours. It will double in bulk noticeably.

Punch the dough down, turn out onto a floured surface, and divide into 4 equal pieces. Let the dough sit at room temperature under a clean dish towel for about 20 minutes. Roll each piece on a floured board until about 5 inches in diameter.

Preheat the oven to 400°F.

Spread a thin layer of marinara sauce on each round of dough, leaving a 1-inch border, and top with the cheese. Transfer each circle of the pizza dough to a baking sheet or pizza stone. Bake for 15 to 18 minutes, or until the cheese starts to bubble and the crusts turn golden brown. Serve hot.

SERVES 4

TIP If you get into making pizza fairly often—and once you realize how easy it is to make your own dough, you might—you'll want to invest in a pizza stone. This low-tech piece of equipment sits on the lowest rack of the oven and heats up as the oven does. Pizza stones, also called baking stones or ceramic baker's tiles, hold heat, not unlike the floor and walls of a traditional pizza oven. When you slide the pizza dough onto the stone, the bottom of the crust cooks quickly and turns extra crispy because the hot stone absorbs the dough's moisture.

You might also want a pizza peel, which is a flat, thin-edged wood or metal tray with a long handle that slips easily under the pizza dough to transfer it to and from the oven. These peels are also great for moving loaves of bread in and out of the oven. Finally, a pizza wheel makes cutting the pizza as easy as one-two-three. Start at the center of the pie and roll the cutter toward the edge.

To freeze the dough, once it's risen and been punched down, wrap it in plastic and put in a freezer bag. Freeze for up to 1 month. To use, let it defrost in the refrigerator overnight. Remove 30 minutes before shaping and baking.

tropical chicken skewers with mango yogurt dipping sauce

I love this recipe because kids can skewer as much chicken or fruit as they like. When we make these in a kids' cooking class, the kids get so creative we're always happily surprised by the variety; no two skewers look alike! Make these first so they can marinate while the kids move on to the pizza or cake.

MARINADE

1 cup pineapple juice

1 cup orange juice

$^1/_2$ cup canola oil

2 tablespoons dark brown sugar

1 tablespoon fresh lemon juice

1 teaspoon salt

$^1/_2$ teaspoon ground allspice

1 small chipotle or other small, hot pepper, such as jalapeño, seeded and chopped (optional)

CHICKEN

1 ripe papaya

$^1/_2$ small ripe pineapple (see Note)

3 boneless, skinless chicken breast halves (5 to 7 ounces each)

12 cherry tomatoes, rinsed

Flavorless vegetable oil spray

Salt and freshly ground pepper

Mango Yogurt Dipping Sauce (recipe follows)

Special equipment: Six 12-inch bamboo skewers, soaked in cold water for at least 30 minutes

To make the marinade, combine the pineapple juice, orange juice, oil, brown sugar, lemon juice, salt, allspice, and chipotle in a small saucepan. Place over medium-high heat and bring to a boil. Reduce the heat and simmer for about 25 minutes, or until thickened and slightly reduced. Remove from the heat and set aside to cool completely.

Peel, halve, and seed the papaya and cut it into 12 pieces.

Cut the pineapple into 12 pieces, similar in size to the papaya.

Cut the chicken into 24 pieces, similar in size to the fruit.

Start threading the chicken, fruit pieces, and tomatoes onto the skewers, alternating as you go, using about 4 pieces chicken, 2 cherry tomatoes, 2 chunks pineapple, and 2 chunks papaya for each skewer. Lay the finished skewers in a large rectangular glass, ceramic, plastic, or other nonreactive dish, deep enough to hold them in a single layer. Pour the cooled marinade over the skewers. Cover and refrigerate for 1 hour.

Prepare a charcoal or gas grill so that the coals or heating elements are medium hot. Off the heat, lightly spray the grate with vegetable oil spray.

Lift each skewer from the marinade and let any excess drip back into the dish. Discard the marinade. Season each skewer with salt and pepper and grill for 5 to 7 minutes per side, turning as needed, until the chicken is cooked through.

Serve the skewers, passing the dipping sauce on the side or pouring it into small individual dishes for each person.

SERVES 6 (OR MORE, DEPENDING ON THE AGE OF THE KIDS)

NOTE: To peel a pineapple, slice off the crown and base. Place the pineapple on one end, and carefully slice off the skin, carving out any of the remaining "eyes" with the tip of the knife. Slice 4 large pieces off the core and then cut those pieces into the desired size.

mango yogurt dipping sauce

Slice both ends from the mango to determine where the seed is located. Peel the skin from the mango with a sharp knife or peeler. Cut the fleshy "cheeks" from each side of the mango by cutting in half lengthwise along the side of the seed. Trim around the mango, following the curve of the seed to remove the remaining flesh. Transfer the flesh to the bowl of a food processor fitted with a metal blade or to a blender.

Add the yogurt, chipotle pepper, lime juice, scallion, and salt and pulse until smooth. Season to taste with pepper and more salt if necessary and pulse once or twice to blend. Serve with chicken skewers. The sauce can be refrigerated for up to 2 days.

MAKES ABOUT 1 1/4 CUPS

1 large ripe mango
1/4 cup plain yogurt
1 small chipotle pepper or other small, hot pepper, such as jalapeño, seeded and chopped (optional)
Juice of 1 lime
1 scallion, thinly sliced
1 teaspoon salt, plus more if needed
Freshly ground pepper

Call the Kids
- Measure the juices and oil
- Mix the ingredients for the marinade
- Cut up the papaya with a blunt knife
- Wash the cherry tomatoes
- Measure the yogurt for the dipping sauce

USE YOUR JUDGMENT
- Pulse the sauce in the food processor

raspberry-filled sugar cookie hearts

These pretty little cookies are a hit at kids' parties because the children like to roll and fill them. They also are an obvious choice for Valentine's Day or Mother's Day. We fill them with raspberry jam, but you could choose another flavor, such as strawberry, apricot, or peach. We like making hearts, but the sugar cookie dough is equally good for any type of roll-and-cut cookie. For a party, you might decide to make the dough ahead of time and let the kids roll, cut, and fill the cookies.

Flavorless vegetable oil spray

3 cups all-purpose flour, plus more
   for dusting

$3/_4$ teaspoon baking powder

$1/_4$ teaspoon salt

1 cup (2 sticks) unsalted butter,
   softened

1 cup granulated sugar

1 large egg

1 tablespoon milk

$1/_4$ teaspoon lemon extract

$1/_4$ cup seedless raspberry jam

Confectioners' sugar

Call the Kids

- Spray the baking sheets with vegetable oil spray
- Measure the flour
- Whisk together the flour, baking powder, and salt
- Beat the butter and sugar
- Add the dry ingredients to the batter
- Roll out the dough
- Cut the hearts from the dough
- Spread the jam on the hearts
- Sandwich the cookies
- Dust the cookies with confectioners' sugar

Preheat the oven to 350°F. Lightly spray 2 baking sheets with flavorless vegetable oil spray or use nonstick baking sheets.

In a medium bowl, whisk together the flour, baking powder, and salt. Set aside.

In the bowl of an electric mixer fitted with the paddle attachment and set on medium-high speed, beat the butter and granulated sugar until light and fluffy. Add the egg and beat until well mixed.

Slowly add the dry ingredients, mixing on medium-low speed, until just incorporated. Add the milk and lemon extract and mix just until the dough comes together.

Turn the dough out onto a lightly floured work surface and divide it into 2 pieces. Using a lightly floured rolling pin, roll each piece about $1/_8$ inch thick. Using a 2- to $2^1/_2$-inch-wide heart-shape cookie cutter, stamp out heart-shape cookies. Gather the dough scraps, reroll, and cut out more cookies.

Put the cookies on the baking sheets and bake for 10 to 12 minutes, or until very lightly browned and just beginning to crisp around the edges. Remove the baking sheets from the oven and let the cookies sit on them for 2 to 3 minutes before removing with a spatula. Cool the cookies on wire racks.

When the cookies are cool, spread half of them with jam and sandwich with the rest. Dust the cookies with confectioners' sugar. The cookies keep in an airtight container for up to 2 days.

MAKES 4 DOZEN COOKIES

flowerpot cakes

This easy, moist chocolate cake lends itself to these flowerpot cakes or can be made as a traditional layer cake. When we give parties at Aux Délices, the kids can't wait to make these and they are wonderfully creative when it comes to decorating the flowerpots with gummy worms and sprinkles.

Preheat the oven to 350°F. Spray 2 clean unglazed (very important) terra-cotta pots, each 4 inches high and 4 inches across at the top, with flavorless vegetable oil spray. Put a small piece of parchment paper in the bottom of each pot to cover the hole.

In a medium bowl, whisk together the flour, baking soda, baking powder, and salt and set aside.

In a small bowl, stir together the boiling water and cocoa.

In the bowl of an electric mixer fitted with the paddle attachment, cream the sugar and butter on medium speed for 5 to 6 minutes, scraping the bowl once during the process, until light and fluffy. Add the eggs one at a time and beat well after each addition.

With the mixer on low speed, add the dry ingredients, alternating with the water-cocoa mixture and beginning and ending with the dry ingredients. Scrape the bowl occasionally while you are adding these ingredients.

Divide the batter evenly between the pots to fill about three quarters of the way.

Line a baking sheet with baking parchment. Put the filled pots on the baking sheet and bake for 40 to 50 minutes, or until the cakes are slightly springy to the touch and a toothpick inserted in the center of a cake comes out clean and dry.

Transfer the pots to wire racks and let the cakes cool completely in the flowerpots. Frost the top of each with the Homestyle Chocolate Frosting or with another favorite frosting. Decorate the cakes with gummy worms, chocolate sprinkles, flower lollipops, and similar candies.

Let the kids dig right into the pots to eat the cakes!

MAKES 2 FLOWERPOT CAKES; SERVES 12

NOTE: The cake batter fills two 8-inch layer cake pans, if you prefer. Bake the cake layers for 30 to 35 minutes. Cool on wire racks and fill and frost as desired.

Flavorless vegetable oil spray

2 cups plus 1 tablespoon all-purpose flour

1 1/2 teaspoons baking soda

1/4 teaspoon baking powder

1/4 teaspoon salt

1 1/2 cups boiling water

3/4 cup unsweetened cocoa powder

1 3/4 cups sugar

3/4 cup (1 1/2 sticks) unsalted butter, softened

3 large eggs

Homestyle Chocolate Frosting (page 187)

Call the Kids

- Spray the pots with vegetable oil spray
- Measure the flour
- Whisk the flour, baking soda, baking powder, and salt
- Beat the sugar and butter
- Add the eggs to the batter
- Add the dry ingredients and water-cocoa mixture to the batter
- Fill the flowerpots
- Measure and mix the frosting
- Frost the cake
- Decorate the flowerpot cakes

backyard summer suppers on the grill

teriyaki grilled salmon ❋ citrus-grilled chicken breasts with mango salsa ❋ grilled corn with basil butter ❋ grilled mushroom stacks ❋ mixed fruit rustic tart

Here are some menu ideas designed for one of my favorite activities, backyard grilling. The pace is relaxed, the food can be eaten at any temperature, and everyone gravitates toward the grill while I cook. This makes outdoor meals casual, movable feasts, enjoyed as they happen. You may decide to grill the chicken alone and save the salmon for another evening, or, if it's a weekend and you've asked friends to join you, grill both. Kids love to prepare the corn for grilling and to build the mushroom stacks. They'll want to help, although don't be surprised if kitchen duty is trumped by a game of kickball or a firefly hunt.

Everyone loves dessert but not a stifling hot kitchen. Make the fruit tart early in the day and then you don't have to worry about dessert at all, until it's time to serve it! By the time dinner is done, the coals will have burned down to a perfect point to grill marshmallows. The kids love this activity almost as much as everyone else will be thrilled with the sweet tart, full of soft, cooked fruit cradled in the tender crust.

teriyaki grilled salmon

Both kids and adults love the mildly sweet-and-sour flavors of teriyaki sauce. This one is fabulous with salmon—it cuts through the richness of the fish—and is equally good with chicken. Making your own teriyaki sauce is easy and allows you to control what's in it, resulting in a better flavor. Toss the salmon on the grill and everyone will be eager for dinner!

In a small bowl, stir together the soy sauce, mirin, ginger, garlic, and brown sugar to make the teriyaki marinade.

Lay the salmon fillets in a shallow nonreactive container and pour the marinade over them. Turn to coat. Cover and refrigerate for at least 1 hour and up to 3 hours.

Prepare a charcoal or gas grill so that the coals or heating elements are medium hot. Off the heat, lightly spray the grate with vegetable oil spray.

Remove the salmon from the marinade. Discard the marinade. Lightly oil the flesh side of the fish with olive oil and season with salt and pepper. Grill the salmon, flesh side down, for 3 to 4 minutes. Rotate the fish 90 degrees on the grill to create a crosshatch effect, and grill for 3 to 4 minutes longer. Turn the salmon over and grill on the skin side for 2 to 3 minutes for medium.

To serve, sprinkle with sesame seeds, if desired.

SERVES 4

NOTE: Mirin is sweetened sake (rice wine) and is sold in supermarkets in the Asian food section.

1 cup soy sauce

1/4 cup mirin (see Note)

2 tablespoons grated fresh ginger

2 garlic cloves, thinly sliced

1 tablespoon brown sugar

4 salmon fillets with skin, 6 to 7 ounces each

Flavorless vegetable oil spray

Olive oil

Salt and freshly ground pepper

Black and white sesame seeds (optional)

Call the Kids

- Measure the soy sauce
- Mix the soy sauce, mirin, ginger, garlic, and sugar
- Pour the marinade over the salmon
- Sprinkle the salmon with sesame seeds

citrus-grilled chicken breasts
with mango salsa

We love the bright, fresh taste citrus gives chicken, and we like salsas in any shape or form. My kids are more than happy to cut up the mango. They're not put off by the messiness, and they always steal pieces of mango to eat while they are cutting it up.

1/2 cup canola oil

Grated zest and juice of 1 orange

Grated zest and juice of 1 lemon

Grated zest and juice of 1 lime

2 garlic cloves, sliced

1/2 jalapeño pepper, seeded and minced

4 boneless, skinless chicken breast halves (5 to 6 ounces each)

Flavorless vegetable oil spray

Salt and freshly ground pepper

Mango Salsa (recipe follows)

Call the Kids

- Measure the oil
- Squeeze the orange, lemon, and lime
- Turn the chicken in the marinade
- Cut the mango with a blunt knife
- Stir together the ingredients for the salsa

In a shallow glass, ceramic, or other nonreactive dish, combine the oil, citrus zests and juices, garlic, and jalapeño. Mix well. Add the chicken and turn once or twice to coat evenly. Cover and refrigerate for at least 3 hours and no longer than 6 hours.

Prepare a charcoal or gas grill so that the coals or heating elements are medium hot. Off the heat, lightly spray the grate with vegetable oil spray.

Lift the chicken breasts from the marinade, letting any excess drip back into the dish. Discard the marinade. Season the chicken with salt and pepper. Grill for 4 to 5 minutes per side, or until the chicken is cooked through.

Serve the chicken with the mango salsa.

SERVES 4

mango salsa

Slice both ends from the mango to determine where the seed is located. Peel the skin from the mango with a sharp knife or peeler. Cut the fleshy "cheeks" from each side of the mango by cutting almost in half lengthwise along the side of the seed. Trim around the mango, following the curve of the seed to remove the remaining flesh from the other sides. Cut the mango into a small dice and put in a medium bowl.

Add the onion, cilantro, lime juice, oil, jalapeño, salt and pepper and mix well. Taste and adjust the seasonings, if necessary. Serve at room temperature or refrigerate for up to 2 days.

MAKES ABOUT 2 CUPS

1 ripe mango

3 tablespoons chopped red onion

2 teaspoons chopped fresh cilantro leaves

1 tablespoon fresh lime juice

1 tablespoon olive oil

1 teaspoon chopped jalapeño pepper (about a quarter of a jalapeño)

$1/4$ teaspoon salt

$1/8$ teaspoon freshly ground pepper

grilled corn with basil butter

For a change from boiled corn-on-the-cob, try grilled corn. For one thing, there's no pot of water to worry about, and kids get a real kick out of corn grilled in the husks after the silks are removed. Fresh, aromatic basil, so abundant in the summer garden, is great mixed with butter to spread on the corn. You could use plain butter or flavor it with a different herb—your choice. The best thing about making herb butter is that you can double or triple the recipe and freeze what you don't use, wrapped in plastic wrap. So, the next time you grill corn or other vegetables, you're all set!

2 cups fresh basil leaves

$1/2$ cup (1 stick) unsalted butter, softened

1 teaspoon grated lemon zest

$1/2$ teaspoon salt

Freshly ground pepper

Flavorless vegetable oil spray

4 ears corn

Call the Kids

- Pick the basil leaves
- Measure the salt
- Process the butter
- Husk the corn
- Brush the corn with the butter

Fill a small saucepan with water and bring to a boil. Set up a small bowl of ice water nearby. Blanch the basil leaves in boiling water for about 30 seconds until wilted yet still bright green. Scoop out with a slotted spoon and transfer to the ice water. When cool, gently squeeze dry in a kitchen towel.

In the bowl of a food processor fitted with a metal blade, process the basil leaves with the butter, zest, and salt until smooth. Taste and season with pepper. Pulse once or twice.

Prepare a charcoal or gas grill so that the coals or heating elements are medium hot. Off the heat, lightly spray the grate with vegetable oil spray.

While the grill is getting hot, remove the husks from the corn without detaching them completely. Remove the silks and discard. Pull the husks up over the corn to encase.

Lay the corn on the grill and cook for 8 to 10 minutes, turning often with tongs, until the kernels are tender. Check by pulling back the corn husks and piercing the kernels with a sharp knife or pressing with your finger. When done, remove the corn from the grill and set aside to cool slightly.

Pull the husks off the corn and top with basil butter. Serve immediately.

SERVES 4

grilled mushroom stacks

This is a colorful, pretty way to serve grilled vegetables. I developed these one day when I had leftovers, and since then I have found that the stacks are practically endlessly versatile. They also are hearty enough for a vegetarian main dish, although I usually serve them as a side. Kids think it's cool that they are skewered with rosemary sprigs, which add flavor.

Prepare a charcoal or gas grill so that the coals or heating elements are hot. Off the heat, lightly spray the grate with vegetable oil spray.

Grill the bell pepper, turning, until charred on all sides, 7 to 8 minutes. Transfer to a bowl and cover with plastic wrap. After about 5 minutes, remove the wrap and rub the blackened skin from the pepper. Cut the bell pepper into quarters, remove the core and seeds, and set aside.

Lay the mushrooms, zucchini, red onion, and tomato slices on a rimmed sheet pan, drizzle with olive oil, and season with salt and pepper. Flip them over and season the other sides. Use tongs to transfer the vegetables to the grill. Grill the mushroom caps for 3 to 4 minutes on each side, or until they are tender. Remove to a plate when done.

Grill the zucchini and onion slices for 3 to 4 minutes per side, or until softened. Remove to a plate when done.

Grill the tomato slices on one side only, for about $1^1/_2$ minutes. Remove to a plate when done.

Build 4 stacks by starting each one with a mushroom cap, gill side up. Top with a slice of the zucchini, onion, tomato, and mozzarella. Add 2 basil leaves and 1 piece of the red bell pepper to each stack. Finally, sandwich with another mushroom cap, gill side facing down.

Trim the bottom leaves from the sprigs of rosemary to expose a bit of the stem and skewer each stack in the center with the rosemary sprig. Serve warm or at room temperature.

SERVES 4

Flavorless vegetable oil spray

1 large red bell pepper

8 small portobello mushroom caps, stemmed and wiped clean

1 medium zucchini, cut on the bias into four $^1/_4$-inch-thick slices

1 medium red onion, peeled and cut into four $^1/_4$-inch-thick slices

1 medium tomato, cut into four $^1/_4$-inch-thick slices

About $^1/_2$ cup extra-virgin olive oil

Salt and freshly ground pepper

4 ounces fresh mozzarella cheese, cut into $^1/_4$-inch-thick slices

8 fresh basil leaves

4 sturdy sprigs rosemary, each about 4 inches long

Call the Kids

- Stem and wipe the mushrooms clean
- Slice the mozzarella with a blunt knife
- Strip the leaves from the rosemary sprigs

mixed fruit rustic tart

This rustic fruit tart is so easy to make, you'll never hesitate when you're in the mood for something sweet and lovely. I like the way it looks with the crust embracing the abundant fruit, and every time I make it, it's a little different, which only adds to its charm. If you have some ice cream on hand, even better!

DOUGH

1 cup (2 sticks) cold unsalted butter, cut into pieces

2¼ cups all-purpose flour, plus more for dusting

½ cup plus 2 tablespoons sugar

1 teaspoon grated lemon zest

1 large egg, lightly beaten

1 large egg yolk, lightly beaten

FILLING

2 firm apples, peeled, cored, and thinly sliced

1 firm, ripe pear, peeled, cored, and thinly sliced

1 nectarine, pitted and thinly sliced

½ pint raspberries

1 tablespoon all-purpose flour

1 tablespoon plus 1 teaspoon sugar

¼ teaspoon ground cinnamon

1 tablespoon milk

To make the dough: In the bowl of a food processor fitted with the metal blade or in the bowl of an electric mixer fitted with the dough hook and set on low speed, combine the butter, flour, sugar, and lemon zest and pulse or mix until the mixture is coarse and resembles wet sand. Add the egg and egg yolk and blend until the mixture comes together and forms a ball. Wrap the dough in plastic and refrigerate for 1 to 2 hours, or until firm.

Preheat the oven to 375°F.

On a lightly floured surface, roll the dough into a large circle that is 12 to 14 inches in diameter. If the edges crack, patch and roll again. Transfer the dough to a baking sheet.

To make the filling: In a large mixing bowl, toss together the apples, pear, nectarine, raspberries, flour, 1 tablespoon of the sugar, and the cinnamon until lightly coated.

Pile the fruit in the center of the dough, leaving a 1½-inch border, then fold up the outer edges of the dough to form a rustic edge and partially cover the fruit. Brush the edge of the dough with the milk and sprinkle with the remaining teaspoon of sugar.

Bake for 35 to 40 minutes, or until the tart is golden brown and the fruit inside is tender. Serve warm or at room temperature.

SERVES 8 TO 10

Call the Kids

- Measure and mix the flour and sugar
- Roll the dough into a large circle
- Peel the apples with a hand-held peeler
- Toss the fruit with the flour, sugar, and spices
- Fold the dough around the fruit

dinnertime

rigatoni with ricotta, tomato, and basil ❋ chili con carne ❋ balsamic, rosemary, and lemon grilled chicken ❋ turkey meatloaf ❋ grilled shrimp satay with ginger and lime ❋ oven-roasted chicken breasts with two simple sauces ❋ pan-seared pork chops with green apple–cranberry compote ❋ pasta primavera ❋

continued on next page →

continued from previous page

oven-barbecued salmon ❋ fish in foil with zucchini ribbons ❋ spaghetti with annabelle's meatballs ❋ aux délices's marinara sauce ❋ grilled spicy red snapper tacos ❋ lemon sole with creamy spinach and mushrooms ❋ barbecued turkey burgers ❋ south-western crab cakes with creamy chipotle sauce ❋ chicken parmesan ❋ grilled vegetable lasagna ❋ grilled flank steak with charred corn, red onion, tomato, and avocado salsa ❋ spring leg of lamb with mint and lemon aioli ❋ cioppino with garlic toasts

I wrote this book because of dinnertime. It's the meal we all face every day with some trepidation or, more often, unfortunately, resignation. Even if we don't sit down at the table for more than ten or fifteen minutes before someone has to rush off, if parents and kids have worked side by side in the kitchen preparing the evening meal, they've spent time together that can't be stolen. Cooking with your kids is a way to extend the meal, to make the process more meaningful, and, along the way, to teach your kids some valuable life lessons while getting them excited about the meal they are about to eat. As I have in every chapter, I've arranged the recipes according to degree of difficulty, and all offer a wide range of styles, flavors, and ingredients. These run the gamut from a simple chili con carne to an elegant lemon sole and a festive leg of lamb. For the most part, they are a little more healthful than the family favorites of yesterday, but just as gratifying and as satisfying.

To make the dinner hour less stressful and more fun for everyone, plan a few meals at the beginning of the week. A well-stocked pantry and updated shopping list (keep a running list on a white board or pad of paper) will help you stay organized. This is a good way to offer the kids choices. They can pick a few recipes from the book and then choose a night when they can help you make them. Just a little forethought will make the process of cooking with the kids relaxing and rewarding.

rigatoni with ricotta, tomato, and basil

My in-laws are Italian and so pasta is a staple of every family gathering. This simple rigatoni dish came out of one of our impromptu weekend get-togethers and it's remained a regular ever since. This is a terrific way to make a simple cheese sauce with fresh ricotta, cream, and basil.

1 pound dry rigatoni pasta

1 tablespoon olive oil

2 garlic cloves, thinly sliced

1 cup grape or cherry tomatoes, halved

$^1/_2$ cup heavy cream

$^1/_4$ cup milk

15 ounces ricotta cheese

$^1/_2$ cup freshly grated Parmesan cheese

$^1/_2$ cup thinly sliced fresh basil leaves

Salt and freshly ground pepper

Call the Kids

- Measure the tomatoes
- Measure the cream and milk
- Grate the cheese
- Sprinkle the cheese on the pasta
- Strip the basil leaves from the sprigs

Cook the pasta in boiling salted water according to the directions on the box.

While the pasta is cooking, heat the olive oil in a large sauté pan over medium heat. Add the garlic and sauté for about 1 minute, or until it just begins to turn golden brown. Add the tomatoes and sauté for 2 to 3 minutes longer. Add the heavy cream and milk and simmer for 1 to 2 minutes. Add the ricotta cheese and stir to combine all of the ingredients.

Drain the pasta, add it to the sauté pan, and toss well to combine. Top with the grated Parmesan and sliced basil and season to taste with salt and pepper.

SERVES 4

chili con carne

Kids tend to like chili, and when they can choose their own toppings, they like it even more. Some nights just call out for chili because it's so warming, hearty, and foolproof. This one, which uses canned beans, comes together in under an hour, and so it's just about perfect for a school-night meal. Leftover chili is terrific for topping hot dogs or for filling tacos.

In a large saucepan or medium pot, heat the oil over medium-high heat until just shimmering. Add the onions and bell pepper and sauté, stirring occasionally, for about 10 minutes, or until the vegetables just begin to brown.

Add the garlic and sauté for 1 minute. Add the ground beef and cook, breaking the meat up with a wooden spoon or long-handled fork as it browns, for about 5 minutes, or until it begins to lose some pinkness. Add the tomatoes with their juice, chili powder, salt, cayenne, and cumin and bring to a simmer. Lower the heat and cook, stirring occasionally, for 30 minutes, or until the meat is cooked through and the flavors have blended.

Add the kidney beans and cook for a few minutes to heat through. Serve topped with sour cream, scallions, or Cheddar, as desired.

SERVES 8

2 tablespoons canola oil
2 medium onions, chopped
1 small green bell pepper, seeded and chopped
5 large garlic cloves, finely chopped
2 pounds lean ground beef
Two 28-ounce cans plum tomatoes, with their juice, coarsely chopped
2 tablespoons chili powder
2 teaspoons salt
$1/2$ teaspoon cayenne
$1/2$ teaspoon ground cumin
Two 16-ounce cans kidney beans, rinsed and drained
Sour cream (optional)
Chopped scallions (optional)
Grated Cheddar cheese (optional)

Call the Kids
- Rinse and drain the kidney beans
- Grate the cheese
- Dish out the sour cream

USE YOUR JUDGMENT
- Stir the chili

balsamic, rosemary, and lemon grilled chicken

If you're like me and find yourself thinking about dinner while you're still having breakfast, this is an ideal recipe. The chicken marinates all day so it's ready for the grill when it's time for dinner. With a little advance planning, you can get dinner on the table very quickly.

1/2 cup balsamic vinegar

1/2 cup canola oil

2 sprigs fresh rosemary leaves, chopped

3 shallots, thinly sliced

3 garlic cloves, thinly sliced

1 lemon, thinly sliced

4 boneless, skinless chicken breasts or split whole chicken breasts

Flavorless vegetable oil spray

Salt and freshly ground pepper

In a shallow nonreactive dish, combine the vinegar, oil, rosemary, shallots, garlic, and lemon. Put the chicken breasts in the dish and turn once or twice to coat thoroughly with the marinade. Cover and refrigerate for 6 to 8 hours or overnight.

Prepare a charcoal or gas grill so that the coals or heating elements are medium hot. Off the heat, lightly spray the grate with vegetable oil spray.

Remove the chicken breasts from the marinade and let most of the marinade drip back into the dish; discard. Season the chicken on both sides with salt and pepper. Grill the chicken on each side for 4 to 5 minutes, depending on the size of the breasts, until cooked through.

SERVES 4

Call the Kids

- Measure the vinegar and oil
- Strip the rosemary leaves from the sprigs
- Turn the chicken in the marinade
- Season the chicken breasts with salt and pepper

turkey meatloaf

We eat this meatloaf at least once a week with lots of ketchup and Sour Cream Mashed Potatoes (page 155). The turkey is a healthful alternative to beef and just as delicious. As a bonus, leftover meatloaf always makes a great sandwich.

Preheat the oven to 350°F. Grease a 9 x 5-inch loaf pan with butter.

In a medium sauté pan, melt the butter over medium heat until it begins to bubble. Add the celery, carrot, shallots, and garlic and sauté, stirring occasionally, for 3 to 4 minutes, or until the vegetables soften but do not color. Remove the pan from the heat and set aside to cool slightly.

In a large bowl, combine the turkey, bread crumbs, eggs, ketchup, cumin, thyme, salt and pepper. Add the sautéed vegetables and mix thoroughly with a large spoon or your hands.

Transfer the mixture to the loaf pan and form into a smooth loaf. Bake for about 1 hour, or until cooked through. Let the meatloaf rest in the pan for about 5 minutes before unmolding, slicing, and serving.

SERVES 6 TO 8

NOTE: To make fresh bread crumbs, process the bread in the bowl of a food processor fitted with a metal blade or in a blender. Two slices of bread yield about 1 cup of crumbs.

6 tablespoons (³/₄ stick) unsalted butter, plus extra for greasing the pan

1 celery rib, diced

1 small carrot, peeled and diced

2 shallots, finely chopped

1 garlic clove, finely chopped

2 pounds ground turkey

2 cups fresh bread crumbs (about 3 to 4 slices of bread; see Note)

2 large eggs

1 scant cup ketchup

1¹/₂ teaspoons ground cumin

1 teaspoon chopped fresh thyme leaves

1 teaspoon salt

1 teaspoon freshly ground pepper

Call the Kids

- Grease the pan
- Measure the bread crumbs
- Measure the ketchup
- Mix the meatloaf ingredients
- Put the meatloaf in the loaf pan

grilled shrimp satay with ginger and lime

Most kids like the taste of shrimp and I haven't met a kid who doesn't like skewers; you get to eat with your hands—without Mom or Dad frowning! To make these grilled skewers even more of a hit, they're served with a peanut sauce so good that finger licking is a must.

1 lime
3 tablespoons olive oil
3 tablespoons soy sauce
2 scallions, white and green parts, finely chopped
1^1/$_2$ teaspoons grated fresh ginger
20 large shrimp (about 1^1/$_2$ pounds), peeled and deveined
Flavorless vegetable oil spray
4 wooden skewers, 8 to 10 inches long
Peanut Dipping Sauce (recipe follows)

Call the Kids
- Mix the marinade
- Peel the shrimp
- Put the shrimp in the marinade
- Cover the dish with plastic
- Soak the skewers
- Thread the skewers with shrimp

Grate the zest from the lime and reserve ^{3}/$_4$ teaspoon. Juice the lime.

In a shallow glass, ceramic, or other nonreactive dish, combine the lime zest and juice, olive oil, soy sauce, scallions, and ginger and mix well. Add the shrimp, turn to coat, and refrigerate for 1 to 2 hours to marinate.

Prepare a charcoal or gas grill so that the coals or heating elements are medium hot. Off the heat, lightly spray the grate with vegetable oil spray.

Soak the wooden skewers in cold water until ready to use.

Remove the shrimp from the marinade and discard the marinade. Thread 5 shrimp onto each skewer and grill for 2 to 3 minutes per side, or until golden brown and just cooked through. Serve immediately with the peanut dipping sauce.

SERVES 4

peanut dipping sauce

2 teaspoons canola oil
3 garlic cloves, minced
1^1/$_2$ teaspoons red pepper flakes
^{1}/$_2$ cup hoisin sauce
3 tablespoons chunky peanut butter
^{1}/$_2$ cup water
Juice of 2 limes

In a small sauté pan, heat the oil over medium heat until shimmering. Add the garlic and sauté for about 1 minute, or until lightly golden brown. Add the pepper flakes and sauté for a few seconds.

Stir in the hoisin sauce, peanut butter, and water, and reduce the heat to medium low so the sauce simmers gently. Add the lime juice and simmer, stirring, for 3 to 4 minutes to allow the flavors to blend.

Let the sauce cool to room temperature. The sauce can be refrigerated for up to 1 week in a lidded container.

MAKES ^{1}/$_2$ CUP

oven-roasted chicken breasts
with two simple sauces

Just about every family has chicken breasts on the menu at least once a week, and my family is no exception. In this recipe, the chicken cooks quickly and simply, but because it is served with one or two sauces, it becomes extra special. These sauces, which can be made days ahead of time and kept in the refrigerator, also taste great with fish and on sandwiches. You could serve the chicken with one sauce one day and then with the other the next, when you're eating leftovers. As far as I am concerned, the more homemade condiments in the refrigerator, the better!

BASIL-LEMON PESTO

1 cup packed fresh basil leaves

3/4 cup olive oil

1/4 cup grated Parmesan cheese

1 teaspoon grated lemon zest

1 garlic clove, sliced

1/2 teaspoon salt

Freshly ground pepper

SWEET TOMATO-THYME MARMALADE

1/4 cup olive oil

1 small onion, diced

1 garlic clove, sliced

4 ripe tomatoes, cored, seeded, and cut into small dice

1 teaspoon chopped fresh thyme

2 tablespoons sugar

1 teaspoon balsamic vinegar

Salt and freshly ground pepper

CHICKEN

4 boneless, skinless chicken breasts

Salt and freshly ground pepper

To make the pesto: In the bowl of a food processor fitted with a metal blade, mix together the basil, olive oil, Parmesan, lemon zest, garlic, and salt. Process until smooth. Season to taste with pepper, and pulse again. You will have about 1 cup. Refrigerate in a tightly lidded container for up to 10 days.

To make the marmalade: In a saucepan set over medium-low heat, heat 2 tablespoons of the olive oil until just shimmering. Add the onions and garlic and sauté for 4 to 5 minutes, or until translucent.

Add the tomatoes, thyme, and sugar, raise the heat to medium, and cook for 30 to 35 minutes, or until the tomatoes are stewed and softened. Add the remaining 2 tablespoons of olive oil and the vinegar and season to taste with salt and pepper. You will have about 2 1/4 cups. Let the sauce cool and refrigerate in a tightly lidded container for up to 10 days. Serve warm or chilled.

Preheat the oven to 375°F.

Season the chicken breasts on both sides with salt and pepper. Lay the breasts in a shallow baking pan and cook for 16 to 18 minutes, or until the chicken is cooked through.

Serve with basil-lemon pesto or sweet tomato-thyme marmalade, or both.

SERVES 4

Call the Kids
- Tear and measure the basil leaves
- Process the pesto
- Stir the marmalade

pan-seared pork chops with green apple–cranberry compote

Typically, when I was growing up, pork was paired with fruit, which makes perfect sense since the mildly sweet meat works so well with it. Today, it's still a familiar and unfailing combination, and one that kids love. In this recipe, I mix the apples with cranberries and sage, which cut the fruit's sweetness with savory accents, making it a hit with adults as well.

Preheat the oven to 350°F.

In an ovenproof sauté pan, heat the oil over medium-high heat until just smoking. Season both sides of the pork chops with salt and pepper and sear for 1 to 2 minutes per side. Transfer the pan to the oven and cook for about 15 minutes, depending on their thickness, until cooked through. Remove from the oven and set aside to rest for about 5 minutes before serving.

Meanwhile, in a medium sauté pan, melt the butter over medium heat. Add the apples, cider, cranberries, and brown sugar, cover the pan, and cook for about 15 minutes, until the apples are soft and wilted.

Uncover the pan, add the sage and balsamic vinegar, and simmer for another 5 minutes or so until all the flavors are combined.

To serve, place a couple of spoonfuls of the compote on each pork chop.

SERVES 4

1 tablespoon olive oil

Four 6-ounce boneless pork chops

Salt and freshly ground pepper

2 tablespoons unsalted butter

3 Granny Smith apples, peeled, cored, and thinly sliced

$3/4$ cup apple cider

$1/3$ cup dried cranberries

2 tablespoons light brown sugar

3 sprigs sage, leaves removed and chopped

2 tablespoons balsamic vinegar

Call the Kids

- Season the pork chops
- Peel the apples with a hand-held peeler
- Measure the apple cider
- Measure the cranberries
- Pull leaves from the sage sprigs
- Spoon the compote over the pork chops

pasta primavera

Nothing reminds me more of spring than this simple pasta dish made with the season's traditional vegetables, asparagus and peas. The sauce, while unmistakably creamy (which kids love), is nice and light at the same time, and the vegetables, which cook in the sauce, imbue it with lovely flavor. This is an elegant dish that comes together in under 30 minutes.

In a large sauté pan, heat the canola oil over medium-high heat until almost shimmering. Add the garlic and sauté for about 1 minute, or until lightly golden brown. Add the carrots and half of the tomatoes and cook for 2 to 3 minutes, until the carrots begin to soften.

Add the stock, bring to a boil, immediately reduce the heat, and simmer for 10 to 12 minutes to reduce slightly.

Meanwhile, cook the pasta in boiling salted water according to the package directions so that the pasta is al dente. Drain, drizzle with olive oil, and set aside until needed.

Add the heavy cream to the reduced stock in the sauté pan and bring the liquid to a boil over medium-high heat. Add the broccoli, sugar snap peas, and asparagus and the remaining tomatoes. Reduce the heat and simmer the sauce for about 5 minutes, or until slightly thickened and the vegetables are tender. Add the grated cheese and season to taste with salt and pepper.

Transfer the pasta to a large serving bowl and toss with the primavera sauce. Taste and adjust the seasonings. Serve immediately.

SERVES 6 TO 8

1 tablespoon canola oil

3 garlic cloves, sliced

3 carrots, peeled and thinly sliced

24 grape or cherry tomatoes, halved

$1^1/_2$ cups chicken or vegetable stock or low-sodium broth

1 pound angel hair pasta

Olive oil

$1^1/_2$ cups heavy cream

3 cups broccoli florets

2 cups sugar snap peas

8 asparagus spears, stalks trimmed and peeled, cut into thirds

3 tablespoons freshly grated Parmesan cheese

Salt and freshly ground pepper

Call the Kids

- Peel the carrots with a hand-held peeler
- Measure the stock
- Measure the broccoli
- Measure the peas
- Measure the cream
- Grate the cheese
- Toss the pasta with the sauce

oven-barbecued salmon

While this sweet-and-sour barbecue sauce is great with tuna, bass, swordfish, or even chicken, when paired with salmon, the combination is near perfect in my mind. Barbecue sauce with salmon is a nice change from the more expected lemon or mustard sauces.

BARBECUE SAUCE

1 cup orange juice

$1/2$ cup red wine vinegar

$1/2$ cup champagne or white wine vinegar, plus more if needed

$1^1/2$ cups sugar

2 tablespoons olive oil

1 medium onion, diced

2 garlic cloves, sliced

One 28-ounce can plum tomatoes, drained

$1/2$ cup ketchup

2 tablespoons packed brown sugar

1 tablespoon Worcestershire sauce

1 teaspoon dry mustard

1 teaspoon grated orange zest

Salt and freshly ground pepper

SALMON

Four 6- to 7-ounce salmon fillets

Salt and freshly ground pepper

In a small saucepan, stir together the orange juice, vinegars, and sugar. Bring to a boil, reduce the heat to medium, and simmer for 50 to 60 minutes, or until thick and syrupy.

In a medium sauté pan, heat the olive oil until almost smoking. Add the onion and garlic and sauté for 3 to 4 minutes. Stir in the tomatoes, ketchup, brown sugar, Worcestershire sauce, and mustard and simmer over medium heat for about 25 minutes, or until thickened.

Add the orange juice reduction and the zest to the tomato mixture and simmer for 8 to 10 minutes, until well blended and slightly thickened. Season to taste with salt and pepper and add 1 to 2 additional tablespoons of champagne vinegar, if necessary. This can be made up to 3 days ahead of time and refrigerated in a tightly closed container.

Preheat the oven to 450°F.

Season the salmon with salt and pepper and put the fillets in a shallow baking dish. Spoon a generous amount of the barbecue sauce on top of the salmon and bake for 10 to 12 minutes for medium, or until they reach the desired degree of doneness.

SERVES 4

NOTE: The salmon can also be grilled. Prepare a charcoal or gas grill so that the heating elements are medium hot. Off the heat, lightly spray the grate with vegetable oil cooking spray. Lightly brush the salmon fillets on both sides with olive oil and season with salt and pepper. Grill the salmon for 3 to 4 minutes. Rotate the fish 90 degrees on the grill to create a cross-hatch effect, and grill for 3 to 4 minutes more. Turn the salmon over, and grill for 2 to 3 minutes for medium. Spoon barbecue sauce over each fillet before serving.

Call the Kids

- Measure the juice and vinegars
- Measure the sugar
- Mix the juice, vinegars, and sugar in the saucepan
- Measure the ketchup
- Season the salmon
- Spoon the sauce on the salmon
  USE YOUR JUDGMENT
- Stir the sauce as it cooks

fish in foil with zucchini ribbons

I have never met a child who didn't like the idea of eating dinner out of a foil pouch because it is sort of like an indoor camping trip. Once the ingredients are prepped, everyone can customize his or her own packet, and anticipate the meal even more happily. As the fish and vegetables steam in the foil, they produce their own juices and everything blends together; the whole thing just smells great when you open the packets. You can substitute cod, striped bass, or any mild, white-fleshed fish for the snapper.

Preheat the oven to 350°F.

Lay 4 pieces of aluminum foil on the counter, each approximately 14 x 12 inches. Distribute the carrot, zucchini, and yellow squash matchsticks near the centers of each piece of foil. Scatter the sliced mushrooms and garlic over the vegetables. Generously season with salt and pepper.

Season each snapper fillet with salt and pepper and put one on top of each pile of vegetables. Place 3 slices of tomato on each fillet.

Drizzle each portion with 2 tablespoons olive oil and sprinkle with thyme.

Bring the 2 longer sides of the foil together over the fish and seal the edges by folding them over, as you would wrap a sandwich or fold a letter. Tuck the sides in, folding them together once or twice to form an airtight seal. Make sure there is some room for air to circulate in the packets and that they're not bursting at the seams. Transfer the packets to 2 baking pans large enough to hold them in a single layer or a rimmed baking sheet and bake for about 25 minutes, or until the fish is cooked through and the vegetables are tender. Check one packet by unwrapping it very carefully; the escaping steam will be hot.

Put a packet on each plate and warn everyone to open them with great care because the steam is very hot. Or, open them before serving, transferring the contents to individual shallow bowls or a serving platter.

SERVES 4

2 small carrots, peeled and cut into matchsticks

1 zucchini, cut into matchsticks

1 yellow squash, cut into matchsticks

16 white mushrooms, thinly sliced

4 garlic cloves, minced

Salt and freshly ground pepper

Four 6- to 7-ounce red snapper fillets

2 ripe tomatoes, cored and thinly sliced

$1/2$ cup extra-virgin olive oil

2 teaspoons chopped fresh thyme leaves

Call the Kids

- Cut the foil sheets
- Peel the carrots
- Divide the vegetables onto the foil
- Put the fish on top of the vegetables
- Put the tomatoes on top of the fish
- Fold the packets

spaghetti with annabelle's meatballs

Since I married her son, Greg's mother, Annabelle, has shared many of her family recipes with me, and I couldn't be happier! The kids and I frequently make these meatballs, but they like it even better when their grandmother comes over and they can make them together. This recipe is especially easy if you make the meatballs ahead of time and reheat them in the sauce.

1 tablespoon olive oil

1 small onion, finely diced

2 garlic cloves, thinly sliced

2 slices day-old (slightly stale) white
    bread, torn into pieces or cubed

1/2 cup milk

1 pound mixed ground pork, beef, and
    veal

2 large eggs

1/2 cup freshly grated Parmesan cheese,
    plus extra for serving

2 tablespoons chopped fresh flat-leaf
    parsley leaves

1 teaspoon salt

1/4 teaspoon freshly ground pepper

2 to 2 1/2 cups Aux Délices's Marinara
    Sauce (recipe follows)

2 to 3 cups oil, for frying

1 pound spaghetti

Call the Kids

- Tear up the bread
- Measure the milk
- Soak the bread in the milk
- Grate the cheese
- Mix the meat with the vegetables,
  bread, eggs, and cheese
- Pull the parsley leaves from the stems
- Make the meatballs

In a medium sauté pan, heat the olive oil over medium heat until almost shimmering. Reduce the heat to medium low, add the onion and garlic, and sauté, stirring occasionally, for 3 to 4 minutes, until softened. Remove from the heat and set aside to cool slightly.

Soak the bread in the milk for 2 to 3 minutes, or until saturated.

In a medium bowl, mix the meat with the sautéed onion and garlic, the bread, any milk not absorbed by the bread, eggs, cheese, parsley, salt, and pepper. Pinch off walnut-size pieces of meat and roll into meatballs between your palms. You will have 10 or 12 meatballs. Cook these as instructed below or freeze. To freeze, lay them in a single layer in a freezer-safe dish and freeze for up to 1 month. Defrost the meatballs in the refrigerator before cooking.

Bring a large pot of salted water to a boil for the pasta. Heat the marinara sauce in a covered saucepan over medium heat until hot, if necessary.

Pour enough oil into a medium-size deep sauté pan to a depth of 1 inch. Heat over medium-high heat until it reaches 350°F. Add 4 to 5 meatballs, one by one, to the pan and fry for about 10 minutes, turning once, or until browned and cooked through. Lift from the oil with a slotted spoon and drain on paper towels. Repeat with the remaining meatballs.

Meanwhile, cook the spaghetti in the boiling water according to the package directions. Drain and toss with 2 cups of the marinara sauce. Add more if necessary or to your taste. Put the sauced pasta in shallow bowls or a serving bowl and top with the meatballs. Serve Parmesan cheese on the side.

SERVES 4 TO 6

NOTE: While the meatballs are fried in this recipe, you could also put them in a baking dish and bake them in a 375°F. oven for about 25 minutes. They won't be as nicely browned, but that won't matter once they are mixed with the sauce.

aux délices's marinara sauce

Before we opened Aux Délices in Greenwich, my husband, Greg, had a restaurant in another Connecticut town, where his customers raved about his marinara sauce. We adopted it at Aux Délices and we use it at home, too. I always have some of this in the freezer to use for a quick pasta dish or for topping pizza, or anytime I need a good red sauce.

In a medium saucepan, heat the oil over medium-high heat until shimmering. Add the onion and sauté, stirring occasionally, for 4 to 5 minutes, or until translucent.

Add the garlic and sauté for a minute or so; do not let it color. Add the tomatoes, sugar, and salt to the saucepan, bring to a simmer, and cook for 15 minutes. Add the oregano, pepper, and red pepper flakes and simmer for another 15 minutes.

Remove from the heat and stir in the butter, scallion, parsley, and Parmesan cheese. Serve immediately or cool completely, cover, and refrigerate for up to 5 days or freeze for up to 2 months.

MAKES ABOUT 3 CUPS

2 tablespoons olive oil

1/2 small white onion, finely diced

1 garlic clove, finely chopped

One 28-ounce can plum tomatoes, tomatoes and juice puréed in a blender or food processor

1 tablespoon sugar

1 teaspoon salt

1/4 teaspoon dried oregano

1/8 teaspoon freshly ground pepper

1/8 teaspoon red pepper flakes

2 tablespoons cold butter

1 scallion, thinly sliced

1 tablespoon chopped fresh flat-leaf parsley leaves

1 tablespoon freshly grated Parmesan cheese

Call the Kids
- Measure the seasonings
  USE YOUR JUDGMENT
- Purée the tomatoes
- Stir the butter, scallions, parsley, and cheese into the sauce

grilled spicy red snapper tacos

Everyone likes food that can be picked up and eaten by hand, which partly explains why children are so fond of tacos. They also like them because, in addition to tasting good, tacos lend themselves to a variety of toppings. When you serve fish in a taco, it's enough of a variation from the norm—which might be a plain fish fillet—that the kids go for it. And they love making their own.

MARINADE

1/2 cup extra-virgin olive oil

Juice of 3 limes (3 to 4 tablespoons)

1/3 cup chopped fresh cilantro leaves

2 tablespoons adobo sauce (see Note)

2 teaspoons salt

1 teaspoon ground cumin

SNAPPER

1 1/2 pounds red snapper fillets

Flavorless vegetable oil spray

Eight 6-inch flour tortillas

Guacamole

Sour cream

Tomato salsa

Lime wedges (optional)

Call the Kids

- Measure the olive oil
- Squeeze the juice from the limes
- Mix the marinade
- Toss the fish with the marinade
- Garnish the tacos

In a small bowl, combine the oil, lime juice, cilantro, adobo, salt, and cumin. Measure and reserve 2 tablespoons of the marinade in a medium bowl.

Lay the fish fillets in a shallow glass, ceramic, or other nonreactive dish. Spoon the marinade over the fish to coat it completely. Set aside at room temperature to marinate for 30 minutes. (Do not let the fish marinate for much longer than this or its texture will be soft.)

Prepare a charcoal or gas grill so that the coals or heating elements are hot. Off the heat, lightly spray the grate with vegetable oil spray.

Grill the snapper for about 4 minutes on each side, or until the snapper is just cooked through and the flesh is opaque. Put the fish on a plate while you grill the tortillas.

Lay the tortillas on the grill and cook for 20 to 30 seconds on each side, or until they begin to turn golden. Stack the tortillas on a plate and cover with foil to keep warm.

Using a fork or your fingers, flake the snapper into bite-size pieces. Toss the fish with the reserved 2 tablespoons marinade. Divide the fish equally among the tortillas. Serve with guacamole, sour cream, tomato salsa, and a squirt of lime juice as desired.

SERVES 4

NOTE: Use the adobo sauce found in cans of chipotle peppers in adobo sauce, which you will need to make the Creamy Chipotle Sauce on page 134. This is readily available in most supermarkets, and is also sold separately in some specialty stores.

lemon sole with creamy spinach and mushrooms

I like the earthiness of mushrooms and shallots with spinach, and a little cream adds a touch of richness to it. Because it's a delicate, mild-flavored fish, lemon sole is a good one to serve kids who are willing to try fish. It is flaky and light, and so passes muster with most kids while still appealing to grown-ups.

In a medium sauté pan, melt the butter over medium heat. Add the shallots and sauté, stirring occasionally, for 4 to 5 minutes, or until they soften. Add the mushrooms and sauté for another 4 to 5 minutes, or until they soften. Add the heavy cream, bring to a boil, reduce the heat, and simmer gently for about 5 minutes, or until the mixture thickens.

Add the spinach leaves and stir for 1 to 2 minutes, until they begin to wilt. Season to taste with salt and pepper. Cover the pan, remove from the heat, and set aside to keep warm.

Season the sole with salt and pepper. In a large sauté pan, heat 1 tablespoon of the olive oil over medium-high heat until smoking. Reduce the heat to medium, add 2 of the fillets, and cook for 3 to 4 minutes on each side, until lightly browned and cooked through. Remove from the pan and set aside on a warm plate, covered with foil, to keep warm. Add the remaining tablespoon of oil to the pan and let it get hot before cooking the remaining 2 fillets. (If you have 2 large sauté pans, by all means have both pans going at once.)

To serve, spoon the spinach mixture onto 4 serving plates. Put a piece of sole on top of the mixture, and drizzle any juices from the pan or plate on top. Serve immediately.

SERVES 4

3 tablespoons unsalted butter
8 shallots, thinly sliced
16 small white mushrooms, sliced
$1^1/_4$ cups heavy cream
6 ounces baby spinach leaves
Salt and freshly ground pepper
Four 6- to 7-ounce lemon sole fillets
2 tablespoons olive oil

Call the Kids
- Wipe the mushrooms clean
- Measure the cream
- Stir the spinach-mushroom mixture
- Season the fillets of sole
- Spoon the spinach-mushroom mixture onto the plates

barbecued turkey burgers

Slathered with barbecue sauce and topped with grilled onions and tomatoes, these burgers make a perfect meal with lots of gusto! They are knife-and-fork burgers—not a bun in sight!

TOPPING

Flavorless vegetable oil spray

2 large red onions

2 large ripe tomatoes

2 tablespoons olive oil

Salt and freshly ground pepper

BURGERS

2 tablespoons unsalted butter

$1/3$ cup finely diced onion

2 garlic cloves, finely chopped

$2^1/2$ pounds ground turkey

2 tablespoons Worcestershire sauce

1 tablespoon chopped fresh flat-leaf parsley leaves

$1^1/2$ teaspoons salt

$1/2$ teaspoon chopped fresh thyme leaves (optional)

$1/4$ teaspoon freshly ground pepper

$3/4$ cup Barbecue Sauce (recipe follows), or store-bought

To cook the onions and tomatoes, prepare a charcoal or gas grill so that the coals or heating elements are medium hot. Off the heat, lightly spray the grate with vegetable oil spray.

Slice the onions and tomatoes crosswise about $1/3$ inch thick. Drizzle them with the olive oil and season with salt and pepper. Grill the onion slices for 3 to 4 minutes, turning once. Keep on the grill until softened. Grill the tomato slices on one side only for 2 minutes. Reserve to use as garnish.

To make the burgers, in a small sauté pan, heat the butter over medium heat until bubbly. Add the onion and garlic and sauté, stirring occasionally, for about 4 minutes, or until soft and translucent. Set aside to cool slightly.

In a large bowl, combine the turkey, Worcestershire sauce, parsley, salt, thyme (if using), and pepper. Add the onion and garlic and mix well with your hands. Form the mixture into 8 patties, each $3/4$ to 1 inch thick and about $3^1/2$ inches in diameter.

Grill the burgers for about 6 minutes. Turn and grill for 4 to 5 minutes longer, or until cooked through. Brush each burger with barbecue sauce and grill for 2 minutes longer.

Serve topped with the grilled onions and tomatoes.

SERVES 8

Call the Kids

- Pull the parsley and thyme leaves from their stems
- Mix the turkey mixture
- Form the turkey into patties

USE YOUR JUDGMENT

- Grill the onions and tomatoes
- Grill the burgers

barbecue sauce

In a nonreactive saucepan, heat the oil over medium heat. Add the onion and garlic and sauté for 3 to 5 minutes, stirring occasionally, until the onion is translucent. Add the bell pepper and cook for 8 to 10 minutes longer, or until soft.

Add the ketchup, molasses, and water and bring to a boil over high heat. Reduce the heat to medium and simmer, uncovered, for about 30 minutes, until the flavors blend.

Stir in the vinegar and simmer for 2 more minutes.

Let the sauce cool to room temperature and transfer it to a lidded container. The barbecue sauce will keep in the refrigerator for about 2 weeks.

MAKES ABOUT 3 CUPS

2 tablespoons olive oil

1 onion, sliced

2 garlic cloves, thinly sliced

1 red bell pepper, seeded and thinly sliced

3 cups ketchup

$^1/_4$ cup molasses

1 cup water

1 tablespoon red wine vinegar

southwestern crab cakes with creamy chipotle sauce

The first time you make these crab cakes you may be surprised at how loosely they hold together. This is because they are more crab than binder, which explains why I am so crazy about them. Fresh bread crumbs are critical—they hold the crab cakes together *and* taste great.

1 pound lump crabmeat

1/2 cup Fresh Mayonnaise (page 51), or store-bought

2 large eggs

3 or 4 scallions, trimmed and sliced on the bias, white and green parts

1/2 orange or red bell pepper, seeded and finely diced

Creamy Chipotle Sauce (recipe follows)

3 tablespoons chopped fresh cilantro

3 cups fresh bread crumbs (see Note, page 117)

2 cups canola oil, for frying

Call the Kids

- Clean the crabmeat
- Mix the chipotle sauce
- Mix the ingredients for the crab cakes
- Make and measure the bread crumbs
- Measure the oil
- Bread the crab cakes

Remove and discard any cartilage or shells from the crabmeat. Reserve.

In a medium bowl, whisk together the mayonnaise, eggs, scallions, bell pepper, 3 tablespoons of the chipotle sauce, and the cilantro. Fold in the crab just until coated with the mayonnaise mixture. Gently fold in 2 cups of the bread crumbs.

With damp hands, form the mixture into 8 crab cakes about 2 1/2 inches in diameter.

Spread the remaining 1 cup bread crumbs in a shallow dish and carefully roll the cakes in the crumbs to coat on all sides. Put the crab cakes on a wax paper–lined tray or plate and refrigerate for up to 2 hours or until set.

Preheat the oven to 350ºF.

In a 10-inch sauté pan, heat the oil over medium-high heat until it registers 350ºF. on a deep-frying thermometer. Fry the crab cakes for 2 to 3 minutes on each side, or until golden brown, working in 2 batches if necessary.

Transfer the fried crab cakes to a baking sheet and bake for 15 minutes, or until heated through. Serve immediately with the remaining chipotle sauce on the side.

SERVES 8

creamy chipotle sauce

1/2 cup Fresh Mayonnaise (page 51), or store-bought

3 to 4 tablespoons adobo sauce (see Note, page 130)

1 tablespoon chopped fresh chives

Few drops fresh lemon juice

In a small bowl, stir together the mayonnaise, adobo sauce, and chives. Add the lemon juice, taste, and add more juice if necessary. Use immediately or cover and refrigerate for up to 7 days.

MAKES A GENEROUS 1/2 CUP

chicken parmesan

The crispy coating on the chicken becomes soft and comforting as the chicken bakes in the marinara sauce. Melted cheese oozing into the piping-hot sauce crowns the dish for a great finish. If the sauce is already made or if you use store-bought, this dish takes minutes from stove to table; and leftovers are great in a sandwich.

Preheat the oven to 350°F.

Season the chicken breasts on both sides with salt and pepper.

Put the flour in a shallow bowl or on a plate, put the beaten eggs in another bowl, and spread the bread crumbs in a third. Dip the chicken first in the flour to coat on both sides and then dip in the egg to coat. Last, dip the chicken in the bread crumbs to coat. As each chicken breast is coated, set it aside on a plate.

In a large sauté pan, heat the oil over medium-high heat until the oil is very hot. Drop a few bread crumbs in the oil and if they sizzle, the oil is hot enough. Cook the chicken for 2 to 3 minutes on each side, or until golden brown. Lift from the pan with tongs or a wide spatula and transfer to a baking dish large enough to hold them in a single layer. Bake for 10 minutes, or until crispy and cooked through.

Take the pan from the oven and spoon the sauce over the chicken to cover. Sprinkle with the grated cheeses. Return to the oven and bake for 5 to 8 minutes longer, until the cheese melts and the sauce is hot. Serve hot.

SERVES 4

4 boneless, skinless chicken breast halves (5 to 6 ounces each)
Salt and freshly ground pepper
1 cup all-purpose flour
3 large eggs, lightly beaten
2 cups panko or seasoned dry bread crumbs
1 cup canola oil
1½ cups Aux Délices's Marinara Sauce (page 129), or store-bought tomato sauce, warmed
1 cup grated Provolone cheese
½ cup freshly grated Parmesan cheese

Call the Kids
- Season the chicken breasts
- Measure the flour
- Beat the eggs
- Measure the bread crumbs
- Measure the oil
- Grate the cheeses

USE YOUR JUDGMENT
- Spoon the sauce over the chicken
- Sprinkle the cheese over the sauce

grilled vegetable lasagna

This delicious three-cheese lasagna is perfect for meat eaters and vegetarians alike. (Yes, your child will one day come home and declare he is a vegetarian. Sometimes it sticks, sometimes it doesn't. This recipe is great in either case.) It requires a little time to assemble, but you can do this in stages and the result is well worth the effort. I suggest tossing the vegetables on the grill the day before, for instance, when you're grilling something else, and then making the lasagna the next day.

Prepare a charcoal or gas grill so that the coals or heating elements are medium hot. Off the heat, lightly spray the grate with vegetable oil spray.

In a shallow bowl, drizzle the zucchini and squash with 6 tablespoons olive oil and season with salt and pepper. Grill the zucchini and squash on a hot grill for 1 to 2 minutes per side, or until tender. Transfer to a plate and set aside or refrigerate overnight.

If you are using no-cook lasagna noodles, skip this step. Otherwise, bring a large pot of salted water to a boil. Cook the lasagna noodles according to the package instructions. Drain, rinse with cold water, drain well, and reserve. (Drizzle them with a little olive oil to prevent sticking, if you desire.)

Meanwhile, in a medium bowl, stir together the ricotta cheese, egg, basil, parsley, 1 teaspoon salt, and $^1/_2$ teaspoon pepper.

Preheat the oven to 400°F.

To assemble the lasagna, spread $^1/_2$ cup marinara sauce in the bottom of a 13 x 9 x 2-inch baking dish. Lay several lasagna noodles over the sauce to cover, cut to fit if necessary. Layer half the grilled zucchini and half of the squash on top of the noodles, spreading them so that they lie as flat as possible. Sprinkle with $^1/_2$ cup of the Parmesan and a third of the Fontina cheese.

Spread half of the ricotta filling mixture over the Parmesan and Fontina and spoon 1 cup marinara sauce over this layer. Repeat the previous steps, starting with more lasagna noodles and finishing with the marinara sauce. Finally, lay lasagna noodles over the sauce, top with $^1/_2$ cup marinara sauce, and the remaining third of Fontina cheese.

Bake for about 60 minutes, or until bubbly and heated throughout. Remove from the oven and let rest for 10 to 15 minutes before cutting into squares and serving.

SERVES 9 TO 12

Flavorless vegetable oil spray

3 medium zucchini, sliced on the bias into $^1/_4$-inch-thick slices

3 medium yellow squash, sliced on the bias into $^1/_4$-inch-thick slices

6 tablespoons olive oil, plus extra for drizzling

Salt and freshly ground pepper

$^3/_4$ pound fresh or dried lasagna noodles or no-cook lasagna noodles

Two 15-ounce containers ricotta cheese

1 large egg, lightly beaten

2 tablespoons chopped fresh basil leaves

2 tablespoons chopped fresh flat-leaf parsley leaves

Aux Délices's Marinara Sauce (page 129), or store-bought sauce, warmed

1 cup freshly grated Parmesan cheese

12 ounces Fontina cheese, grated

Call the Kids

- Mix the ricotta cheese filling
- Tear the herbs
- Grate the cheeses
- Ladle the marinara sauce into the pan
- Layer noodles, vegetables, and cheese

grilled flank steak with charred corn, red onion, tomato, and avocado salsa

This is an exceptionally easy marinade that the kids can mix themselves and that infuses the flank steak with good but never strong, pungent flavors. It's a good exercise to encourage the kids to smell the vinegar and mustard for the marinade and realize that while the flavors might not appeal to them on their own, the sum of the parts results in a delicious meal.

I find that thin, grilled flank steak appeals to kids more than thick, chewy cuts and so we work it into our summer menus. It cooks quickly, smells great, and is terrific with the corn salsa. Plus, any leftovers are excellent in sandwiches. I serve the salsa with flank steak but also with chicken, pork, and even with quesadillas.

1 cup canola oil

$1/2$ cup red wine vinegar

2 teaspoons dry mustard

2 teaspoons Worcestershire sauce

1 teaspoon salt, plus more for
  seasoning

$1/4$ teaspoon cracked black pepper

Pinch of cayenne pepper

One $1^1/_2$-pound flank steak

Flavorless vegetable oil spray

Freshly ground pepper

Charred Corn, Red Onion, Tomato,
  and Avocado Salsa (recipe follows)

Call the Kids

- Measure the oil and vinegar
- Mix the marinade ingredients
- Pour the marinade over the steak
- Husk the corn
- Brush the corn with oil
- Rub the charred skin from the red bell pepper (the jalapeño is too hot for kids)
- Dice the avocado with a blunt knife
- Toss the salsa

In a small mixing bowl, whisk together the oil, vinegar, mustard, Worcestershire sauce, salt, cracked black pepper, and cayenne pepper.

Put the steak in a shallow glass, ceramic, or other nonreactive dish. Pour the marinade over the steak and turn the meat to coat thoroughly. Cover and refrigerate for at least 6 hours or overnight.

Prepare a charcoal or gas grill so that the coals or heating elements are medium hot. Off the heat, lightly spray the grate with vegetable oil spray.

Lift the flank steak from the dish and let the excess marinade drain off it. Discard the marinade. Season the steak with salt and freshly ground pepper and grill for 5 to 6 minutes on each side for medium rare. Let the steak rest for at least 5 minutes before slicing across the grain.

Serve with the salsa.

SERVES 4

charred corn, red onion, tomato, and avocado salsa

Prepare a charcoal or gas grill so that the coals or heating elements are medium hot. Off the heat, lightly spray the grate with vegetable oil spray.

Brush the corn with 1 tablespoon olive oil and grill, turning as needed, for about 8 minutes, or until charred evenly on all sides. Remove and set aside on a cutting board to cool. Keep the grill on.

When the ears are cool enough to handle, cut the corn kernels from the cobs by standing each ear on its end on the cutting board and slicing the kernels from the lower half of the cob. It is safer to remove only half the kernels at one time and to work from the other half of the cob. Turn the cob over and slice off the lower half of the kernels. Reserve the kernels and discard the cobs.

Grill the bell pepper, turning, until charred on all sides, 7 to 8 minutes; grill the jalapeño until charred, 3 to 4 minutes. Transfer both to a bowl and cover with plastic wrap. After about 5 minutes, remove the wrap and rub the blackened skin from the peppers. Halve, remove the membranes, seed the peppers, and then cut into a small dice.

Drizzle the onion and tomato slices with 2 to 3 tablespoons olive oil and season with salt and pepper. Grill the onion slices for 3 to 4 minutes on each side, or until charred and softened. Grill the tomato slices for 2 to 3 minutes on one side, or until softened. Transfer to a cutting board and, when the onion and tomato are cool enough to handle, cut into a small dice.

In a glass, ceramic, or other nonreactive mixing bowl, mix the corn, peppers, onion, and tomato. Add the avocado, cilantro, cumin, 1/3 cup olive oil, and lime juice. Toss gently and season with salt and pepper to taste. Serve at room temperature.

MAKES ABOUT 3 CUPS

TIP To dice an avocado, slice the avocado in half lengthwise and rotate just a little to separate the halves. Carefully insert the blade (not the tip) of a small, sharp knife into the seed and gently twist to remove. Hold a pitted avocado half in your palm. With a small, sharp knife, first make 1/4-inch-thick vertical and then similar horizontal cuts in the flesh. Take care not to pierce the skin. With a spoon, gently remove the avocado dice from the skin.

Flavorless vegetable oil spray

3 ears fresh corn, husked

About 2/3 cup extra-virgin olive oil

1 red bell pepper

1 small jalapeño pepper

1 small red onion, cut into 1/4-inch-thick slices

1 small tomato, cut into 1/4-inch-thick slices

Salt and freshly ground pepper

1 avocado, peeled, pitted, and diced (see Tip)

2 tablespoons chopped fresh cilantro leaves

1 1/2 teaspoons ground cumin

1 tablespoon plus 1 teaspoon fresh lime juice

spring leg of lamb with mint and lemon aioli

Leg of lamb may not be a dish you would make on an ordinary weeknight, but for Easter, Mother's Day, or any other special occasion, it's perfect. I like to roll a boned leg around a simple herb filling and roast it. This is actually easy to do and the roast cooks evenly and slices very nicely when it's done. The minty aioli is a breeze to whip up and tastes just wonderful with the lamb.

One 4-pound boned and butterflied leg
  of lamb
Salt and freshly ground pepper
Leaves from 2 sprigs fresh rosemary,
  chopped
Leaves from 3 sprigs fresh mint,
  chopped
4 garlic cloves, thinly sliced
Mint and Lemon Aioli (recipe follows)

Call the Kids

- Sprinkle herbs and garlic over
  the lamb
- Help tie the lamb
- Pick mint leaves for the aioli
- Mix the aioli ingredients
- Add the oil to the aioli

Lay the lamb on the counter, spreading it as flat as possible. Season the inside of the lamb with salt and pepper and then sprinkle with the rosemary and mint leaves and garlic slices.

Loosely roll the lamb and tie it along its length with butcher's twine at 1-inch intervals. Put in a roasting pan, cover, and refrigerate for 6 to 8 hours or overnight.

Remove the lamb from the refrigerator 30 minutes before roasting. Preheat the oven to 350°F.

Season the outside of the lamb with salt and pepper. Roast for approximately 1 1/2 hours, or until a meat thermometer inserted in the meatiest part registers 120°F. for a nice rare leg or 125°F. to 130°F. for medium rare.

Remove the leg from the oven, and cut off and discard the twine. Let the lamb rest for 15 to 20 minutes before slicing. Serve with the aioli on the side.

SERVES 6 TO 8

mint and lemon aioli

Fill a small bowl with ice and water and have it ready.

Bring a small pan of water to a boil over medium-high heat. Add the mint leaves and blanch for about 10 seconds. Drain the leaves and immediately submerge in the ice water to stop the cooking. Lift the leaves from the water and gently squeeze excess water from them.

Transfer the leaves to the bowl of a food processor fitted with the metal blade or to a blender. Add the egg yolks, garlic, and mustard. Pulse 2 or 3 times to mix.

With the motor running, add the oil, drop by drop. When $1/4$ cup of the oil has been incorporated, add the oil a little more quickly, but do not pour it in a steady stream. Go slowly.

When all the oil is incorporated and the aioli is emulsified, add the lemon juice and mix. Stop the machine and season to taste with salt and pepper.

Scrape the aioli into a small bowl or other container, cover, and refrigerate until ready to use or for up to 3 days. Stir before serving.

MAKES ABOUT 1 CUP

$1^{1}/_{2}$ cups packed fresh mint leaves
   (from 1 large bunch)
2 large egg yolks
2 garlic cloves, coarsely chopped
1 teaspoon Dijon mustard
1 cup olive oil
Juice of $1/_{2}$ lemon
Salt and freshly ground pepper

cioppino with garlic toasts

Don't be intimidated by the long list of ingredients. This is the best one-pot seafood casserole you can make, and putting it together is a breeze—especially if you've prepared some or all of the vegetables a few hours ahead and refrigerated them. You might want to explain to the kids that cioppino originated in San Francisco when Italian immigrants were looking for a taste of home and a way to use the bounty of the Pacific. While you may think this dish more appropriate for older kids because of all the seafood, if you start your kids early they will develop a taste for this simple yet sophisticated dish. And everyone loves the garlic toasts that so naturally go with it.

$1/4$ cup olive oil

1 medium onion, diced

4 garlic cloves, minced

1 bay leaf

1 teaspoon dried oregano

$1/2$ teaspoon red pepper flakes

$1^1/2$ green bell peppers, seeded, ribs removed, and diced

1 small fennel bulb, halved, cored, and diced

2 tablespoons tomato paste

2 cups dry white wine

4 cups chicken stock or low-sodium broth

One 28-ounce can chopped plum tomatoes with juice

Two 8-ounce bottles clam juice

Salt and freshly ground pepper

12 to 18 small clams in their shells, well washed and cleaned

12 to 18 mussels in their shells, well washed and cleaned

1 pound medium shrimp, peeled and deveined

12 medium sea scallops

8 ounces lump crabmeat, cleaned and picked through for pieces of shell

$1/4$ cup chopped fresh flat-leaf parsley

3 tablespoons chopped fresh basil leaves

Garlic Toasts (recipe follows)

In a large, heavy pot, heat the olive oil over medium-high heat until almost smoking. Add the onion, garlic, bay leaf, oregano, and red pepper flakes. Sauté over medium heat, stirring occasionally, for 5 to 6 minutes, or until the onion begins to soften.

Add the bell peppers and fennel and sauté for 3 to 4 minutes longer. Add the tomato paste, stir for 1 minute, and then add the wine. Bring to a simmer and cook for about 6 minutes, or until almost reduced by half. Add the chicken stock, tomatoes with their juice, and clam juice and season to taste with salt and pepper. Simmer for 30 minutes.

Add the clams and mussels to the pot and cook and stir until their shells open. After 10 minutes, discard any that do not open. Add the shrimp, scallops, and crabmeat and stir until the shrimp and scallops are cooked through, a couple of minutes. Discard the bay leaf, stir in the parsley and basil, and adjust the seasoning, if necessary.

Serve the cioppino in large soup bowls with the garlic toasts on the side.

SERVES 6 TO 8

garlic toasts

Preheat the broiler.

Slice the baguette into 20 to 24 slices, each about $1/2$ inch thick. Lay the slices in a single layer on a baking sheet.

In a small bowl, stir together the butter and the garlic. Brush the butter on each slice of bread and sprinkle each side with salt and pepper. Broil for 2 to 3 minutes, or until golden brown.

1 small baguette, about 12 inches long

2 tablespoons unsalted butter, melted

1 garlic clove, finely minced

Salt and freshly ground pepper

Call the Kids

- Measure the oil
- Clean the clams and mussels
- Peel the shrimp
- Pick through the crabmeat
- Brush the toasts with garlic butter

vegetables and salads

sugar snap peas with mint and lemon ❋ glazed baby carrots ❋ roasted asparagus with parmesan cheese ❋ green beans with pine nut butter ❋ zucchini and corn sauté ❋ asian vegetable stir-fry ❋ apple-raisin slaw ❋ panzanella ❋ sour cream mashed potatoes ❋ ginger and orange sweet potato mash ❋ twice-baked potatoes ❋ grilled sweet potatoes with chipotle lime vinaigrette ❋ vegetable fried rice ❋ "hold the anchovies" caesar salad ❋ grilled corn ratatouille ❋ buttermilk onion rings

This is a tough subject. It's a cliché that children are not supposed to like vegetables, but in my experience that's far from the truth. Most kids are just fine with most vegetables, and if not, I've come up with ideas that make these side attractions a little more intriguing: green beans with nut butter, for example; grilled sweet potatoes; or asparagus with cheese. Kids tend not to like overcooked or canned vegetables, which can be listless and flavorless, but some kids love properly seasoned fresh vegetables with a little butter or olive oil. Everyone likes potatoes and just about everyone likes salad. They're all here. There's nothing juvenile about any of these recipes. In fact, that's the point: dishes the entire family enjoys.

sugar snap peas with mint and lemon

Just a little mint and lemon zest turns already popular sugar snap peas into a very special side dish. If you must use frozen sugar snap peas, go ahead, but fresh are usually easy to find.

Fill a bowl with ice and water. In a saucepan filled with boiling water set over medium-high heat, blanch the sugar snap peas for 3 to 4 minutes, or until bright green and still a little crispy. Submerge immediately in the ice water and drain.

In a sauté pan, heat the oil over medium-high heat until just shimmering. Add the garlic and sauté for 1 minute. Add the peas, mint, and lemon zest, and toss for 2 to 3 minutes, or until heated through. Season to taste with salt and pepper. Transfer the peas to a serving dish.

SERVES 4

TIP When you submerge blanched vegetables in ice-cold water, you complete a process. Vegetables are blanched in boiling water for a relatively short period of time to soften them, not to cook them completely. Once the vegetables are lifted from the boiling water, they are plunged in ice water to set their color so it stays bright, and to set the texture. In professional kitchens, this is known as shocking or refreshing. The blanched and shocked vegetables are then usually cooked further, although they may be added to salads or served with dips without any more cooking. Many vegetables are blanched and shocked before they are frozen.

1 pound fresh sugar snap peas, trimmed and strings removed
1 tablespoon olive oil
1 garlic clove, minced
$1/3$ cup loosely packed chopped mint leaves (10 to 12 leaves)
2 teaspoons grated lemon zest
Salt and freshly ground pepper

Call the Kids
- Pull the strings from the sugar snap peas
- Pull the mint leaves from their stems
- Zest the lemon
- Fill a bowl with ice and water

glazed baby carrots

Simple, simple, simple. This recipe is about as easy as it gets, but it's so good I had to include it. Kids love these glazed carrots because they are sweet, and parents like them because they aren't *too* sweet! If you have trouble getting your kids to eat vegetables, problem solved.

2 tablespoons unsalted butter
1 pound baby carrots, peeled (see Note)
2 tablespoons sugar
2 cups chicken stock or low-sodium broth
$1/4$ teaspoon salt
$1/8$ teaspoon freshly ground pepper

Call the Kids

- Peel the carrots
- Measure the sugar
- Measure the stock

In a shallow saucepan, melt the butter over medium heat until it bubbles. Add the carrots and sauté for about 2 minutes. Add the sugar and sauté for another minute.

Add the stock, bring to a boil over medium-high heat, reduce the heat to medium, and simmer for about 20 minutes, or until the liquid is almost evaporated and the carrots are soft. Season with the salt and pepper and serve hot.

SERVES 4 TO 6

NOTE: Buy small, fresh baby carrots if you can find them. Otherwise, substitute the already-peeled little carrots sold in plastic bags in the supermarket. These work well.

roasted asparagus with parmesan cheese

Steamed asparagus is good, but roasted asparagus is better! Some of the tips get a tiny bit crispy and the rest of the stalk cooks to tender perfection. I particularly like asparagus with Parmesan cheese, which in this recipe bubbles and browns and literally melts in your mouth. Kids like every-thing better when it's topped with cheese, and asparagus is no exception.

20 medium asparagus spears (about
   1 pound), tough ends snapped off
2 tablespoons extra-virgin olive oil
$1/4$ teaspoon salt
$1/8$ teaspoon freshly ground pepper
2 tablespoons freshly grated Parmesan
   cheese

Preheat the oven to 450°F.

Lay the asparagus in a single layer on a rimmed baking sheet, drizzle with the olive oil, and sprinkle with the salt and pepper. Roast for about 15 minutes, shaking the pan once or twice during the roasting, until just tender.

Remove from the oven and sprinkle with the Parmesan cheese. Return to the oven for about 5 minutes, or until the cheese melts and turns golden brown. Serve immediately.

SERVES 4

Call the Kids
- Break the ends off the asparagus
- Drizzle the asparagus with oil
- Sprinkle with cheese

green beans with pine nut butter

I buy green beans often because the kids like them and because fresh beans are nearly always avail-able in the market. I came up with this recipe that uses pine nut butter as a twist from dressing the beans with plain butter, plus it is a nice excuse to try long, slender French beans.

10 ounces French green beans
   (see Note)
3 tablespoons unsalted butter
$1/4$ cup pine nuts
1 tablespoon balsamic vinegar
Salt and freshly ground pepper

In boiling salted water, blanch the green beans for 3 to 4 minutes, or until tender. Drain.

In a small saucepan, melt the butter over medium heat until it begins to bubble. Add the pine nuts and cook for 3 to 4 minutes, or until the butter begins to brown. Add the vinegar and season with salt and pepper.

Put the beans on a platter and spoon the pine nut butter on top.

SERVES 6

NOTE: French green beans are long, slender beans. They are often called *haricots verts*.

Call the Kids
- Measure the butter
- Measure the pine nuts

zucchini and corn sauté

Both corn and zucchini, easy to find all year long, are especially good in the summer and have a natural affinity for each other, as demonstrated in this fresh-tasting dish zipped up with a little garlic and cumin. When I cook with my kids, I like to teach them about the natural order of things, including being aware of when fruits and vegetables are in season. Corn in particular is never better than in the summertime and so we love to make this when we can get it fresh from a farmers' market. I confess this is very good, too, made with frozen corn kernels.

In a large sauté pan, heat the oil over medium heat. Add the garlic, reduce the heat to low, and cook for about 1 minute, or until the garlic is golden brown.

Add the zucchini, raise the heat to medium, and sauté for 6 to 8 minutes. Add the corn and cook for 3 to 4 minutes longer, or until the corn is cooked and the zucchini is softened. Add the scallions and cumin and sauté for 1 minute longer to soften the scallions a little. Add the stock and bring to a simmer.

Season with cilantro and salt and pepper to taste. Serve hot.

SERVES 4

2 tablespoons olive oil

1 garlic clove, thinly sliced

1 pound zucchini, ends trimmed, thinly sliced (1 large zucchini)

$1^1/_2$ cups fresh or frozen and thawed corn kernels

4 scallions, trimmed, white and green parts thinly sliced

$^1/_2$ teaspoon ground cumin

$^1/_2$ cup chicken stock, low-sodium broth, or water

$^1/_4$ cup chopped fresh cilantro leaves

Salt and freshly ground pepper

Call the Kids

- Measure the stock
- Measure the corn kernels
- Season the dish with salt and pepper

asian vegetable stir-fry

Everything gets tossed together in one pan and cooked quickly. Nothing could be easier; and kids seem to love all things stir-fried, especially when flavored with a little soy sauce.

2 tablespoons sesame oil or olive oil

2 carrots, peeled and cut into matchsticks

1 small red or yellow bell pepper, cored, seeded, and cut into matchsticks

1 garlic clove, thinly sliced

2 cups broccoli florets

1 cup snow peas, trimmed

$1/2$ cup chicken or vegetable stock, low-sodium broth, or water

4 ounces white mushrooms, sliced (about $1/2$ cup)

2 tablespoons soy sauce, or to taste

1 teaspoon sesame seeds (optional)

Salt and freshly ground pepper

In a large sauté pan, heat the oil over medium-high heat until just shimmering. Reduce the heat to medium, add the carrots, bell pepper, and garlic, and sauté for 2 to 3 minutes.

Add the broccoli and snow peas and sauté for 1 minute longer, or until the snow peas start to soften. Add the stock and mushrooms, bring to a simmer, and cook for 5 to 6 minutes, or until the broccoli softens.

Add the soy sauce and sesame seeds, if using. Season to taste with salt and pepper and additional soy sauce if necessary. Serve hot.

SERVES 4 TO 6

Call the Kids

- Peel the carrots with a hand-held peeler
- Measure the broccoli
- Trim and measure the snow peas
- Measure the chicken stock

apple-raisin slaw

A colorful and crunchy slaw, this is tossed with a light, tangy yogurt dressing instead of the more expected mayonnaise-based one. The sunflower seeds may be the crowning touch, but the apples and raisins play a sweet role in ensuring this is a hit with every member of the family. (P.S. Toasted sunflower seeds make a great snack!)

In a large bowl, toss together the cabbages, carrot, apple, raisins, and sunflower seeds.

To make the dressing, in a small bowl, whisk together the yogurt, dill, oil, vinegar, sugar, and salt until well mixed. Season to taste with pepper.

Spoon the dressing over the slaw and gently toss to coat lightly. Taste and adjust the seasoning, if necessary.

MAKES 6 CUPS

NOTE: To toast the sunflower seeds, spread them in a small, dry skillet and toast over medium heat, stirring once or twice, for about 1 minute, or until the seeds darken a shade and are fragrant. Transfer to a plate to cool before using.

SLAW
$2^1/_2$ cups shredded red cabbage (about $^1/_4$ small head)

$2^1/_2$ cups shredded Savoy cabbage (about $^1/_4$ small head)

$^1/_2$ cup grated peeled carrot

$^1/_2$ Granny Smith apple, peeled, cored, and finely sliced

$^1/_4$ cup raisins

$^1/_4$ cup raw, unsalted sunflower seeds, toasted (see Note)

DRESSING
$^3/_4$ cup plain yogurt

2 tablespoons chopped fresh dill

1 tablespoon extra-virgin olive oil

1 tablespoon sherry vinegar

2 teaspoons sugar

$^3/_4$ teaspoon salt

Freshly ground pepper

Call the Kids
- Peel the carrot and the apple with a hand-held peeler
- Measure the raisins and seeds
- Toss the slaw
- Measure the yogurt
- Mix the dressing
- Toss the slaw and the dressing

panzanella

When I tried this simple bread and tomato salad one day, my kids were more than enthusiastic. We all like how the bread absorbs the juices from the tomato, the olive oil, and the garlicky vinegar. We constantly eat the fantastic fresh tomatoes available in Connecticut during the summer months and so I am always on the lookout for ways to use them.

12 ounces hearty Italian bread

$1/3$ cup red wine vinegar

2 small garlic cloves, sliced

Salt

$1/2$ cup extra-virgin olive oil

1 cup packed julienned or torn basil leaves (see Note)

4 medium-size ripe tomatoes, peeled, cored, and cut into medium dice

1 large red onion, thinly sliced

Freshly ground pepper

Remove the crusts from the bread and cut into 1-inch cubes. You will have about 6 cups.

In a large bowl, whisk together the vinegar, garlic, and 1 teaspoon salt until the salt dissolves. Whisk in the olive oil and basil.

Add the bread, tomatoes, and onion and toss to combine. Season to taste with salt and pepper. Let the panzanella sit at room temperature for at least 30 minutes before serving.

SERVES 6

NOTE: To julienne, lay the leaves one on top of the other, 5 or 6 at a time. Roll into a cylinder and thinly slice crosswise.

Call the Kids

- Measure the vinegar
- Measure the oil
- Pick the basil leaves from their stems
- Mix the dressing
- Pour the dressing over the salad

sour cream mashed potatoes

When you and the kids are in the mood for a super comfort food, it doesn't get any better than these smooth, creamy potatoes. Let's face it: Sometimes mashed potatoes need to be mixed with nothing fancier than butter and sour cream. When I was a kid I used to put tons of butter and mounds of sour cream on baked potatoes, and I have never lost the pleasure of that taste memory. The olive oil rounds out the flavor and we like to top these with snipped chives, chopped parsley, crumbled crispy bacon, or sautéed onions or shallots—or all of the above!

Put the potatoes in a large saucepan and add enough cold water to cover by an inch or two. Add about a teaspoon of salt and bring to a boil over high heat. Reduce the heat to medium high and simmer for 30 to 35 minutes, or until the potatoes are tender when pierced with a fork or small knife. Drain.

In the bowl of an electric mixer fitted with the whisk attachment, beat the potatoes on low to medium speed. While they are mixing, add the sour cream, butter, and oil. Stop the machine to scrape down the sides of the bowl several times. Season with salt and pepper. Sprinkle with desired toppings. Serve immediately while still hot.

SERVES 6

2^1/$_2$ pounds Russet potatoes, peeled and cut into medium dice
Salt
^{2}/$_3$ cup sour cream
4 tablespoons (^{1}/$_2$ stick) unsalted butter, softened
2 teaspoons extra-virgin olive oil
Freshly ground pepper

TOPPING IDEAS
Snipped fresh chives
Chopped fresh flat-leaf parsley leaves
Crumbled crispy bacon
Sautéed onions or shallots

Call the Kids

- Rinse the potatoes under running water
- Measure the sour cream, butter, and oil
- Add the sour cream, butter, and oil to the potatoes
- Sprinkle the topping on the potatoes

ginger and orange sweet potato mash

When the winter holidays arrive, I make these smooth mashed sweet potatoes. Ginger and orange are wholly compatible with the naturally sweet tubers and bring to mind the traditional flavors of the season. Don't wait for Thanksgiving to try them, though—they are that good.

2¹/₂ pounds (3 large) sweet potatoes
   or yams
2 tablespoons unsalted butter
2 tablespoons light brown sugar
¹/₂ teaspoon salt
¹/₈ teaspoon ground cinnamon
¹/₈ teaspoon grated nutmeg
¹/₈ teaspoon ground ginger
¹/₈ teaspoon grated orange zest

Preheat the oven to 350°F.

Put the sweet potatoes on a baking sheet and bake for about 1 hour, or until very soft.

Slice the potatoes in half, scoop out the flesh, and transfer to a medium bowl. Discard the skins. Add the butter and mash with a fork or potato masher.

Add the brown sugar, salt, cinnamon, nutmeg, ginger, and zest and mix well. Serve immediately while still warm.

SERVES 4 TO 6

NOTE: This recipe can be doubled and be made a day ahead of time. Cool, cover, and refrigerate. Reheat in a casserole in a 350° F. oven for about 45 minutes or until heated through.

Call the Kids

- Rinse the potatoes under running water
- Add the butter to the potatoes
- Mash the potatoes
- Add the brown sugar and salt
- Add the spices
- Mash again

twice-baked potatoes

Kids are fascinated by these baked potatoes because they combine two of their favorite potato dishes: baked and mashed. The idea of spooning the filling back into the skins intrigues them—and of course eating them is an easy deal.

Preheat the oven to 400°F.

Put the potatoes on a baking sheet and bake for 1 hour, or until very tender when pierced with a fork or small knife. Remove from the oven and allow to cool for about 10 minutes, but do not turn off the oven.

Cut the potatoes in half lengthwise and carefully scoop out the flesh. Reserve the potato skins and flesh separately.

Transfer the potato flesh to the bowl of an electric mixer fitted with the whisk attachment. Whip the potatoes on medium speed and as they are being whipped, add the cream, $1/4$ cup of the cheese, the oil, salt, and pepper. Mix until smooth.

Spoon the whipped potatoes into the 4 potato skins that look the best. Sprinkle the tops with the remaining tablespoon of cheese. Set the filled potato skins on the baking sheet and return to the oven for about 5 minutes, or until golden brown. Serve hot.

SERVES 4

TIP When you make twice-baked potatoes or any time you bake a potato, you will end up with potato skins. Everyone loves them. They taste best with a little potato flesh still clinging to the skins—about $1/8$ inch. Cut the skins of potato halves lengthwise in half again. Brush them with olive oil or softened butter (or both), sprinkle with grated cheese and salt and pepper, and broil until golden brown and a little crispy around the edges. Serve these hot with a variety of toppings, including sour cream, chopped scallions, guacamole, salsa, grated Cheddar cheese, crumbled blue cheese, crumbled bacon, chopped sun-dried tomatoes, and chopped fresh herbs.

3 large baking potatoes, washed

$1/4$ cup heavy cream

$1/4$ cup plus 1 tablespoon freshly grated Parmesan cheese

2 tablespoons extra-virgin olive oil

$1/2$ teaspoon salt

$1/8$ teaspoon freshly ground pepper

Call the Kids

- Rinse the potatoes under running water
- Measure the cream
- Grate and measure the cheese
- Whip the potatoes
- Add the cream, cheese, and oil to the potatoes
- Fill the potato skins

USE YOUR JUDGMENT

- Scoop the potato flesh from the skins

grilled sweet potatoes with chipotle lime vinaigrette

Although sweet potatoes are traditional in fall and winter, we enjoy eating them all year long. When we slice them and toss them on the grill, they instantly become summer food. The lime vinaigrette soaks into the potatoes, which take on its great smoky, citrusy flavor.

$2^{1}/_{2}$ pounds (3 large) sweet potatoes, washed

Salt

Flavorless vegetable oil spray

Juice of 1 lime

$^{1}/_{4}$ cup extra-virgin olive oil, plus more for brushing on potatoes

3 tablespoons adobo sauce (see Note, page 130)

Freshly ground pepper

3 scallions, trimmed, white and green parts thinly cut on the bias

Call the Kids

- Rinse the potatoes under running water
- Peel the cooled potatoes
- Squeeze the lime
- Measure the oil
- Mix the vinaigrette
- Brush the potato slices with oil
- Spoon the vinaigrette over the potatoes

Put the potatoes in a large pot and add enough cold water to cover by an inch or two. Add about a teaspoon of salt and bring to a boil over high heat. Reduce the heat to medium and simmer for 30 to 35 minutes, or until the potatoes feel tender when pierced with a fork. (Do not cook the potatoes any longer; they will cook further on the grill.) Drain and set aside to cool.

Prepare a charcoal or gas grill so that the coals or heating elements are medium hot. Off the heat, lightly spray the grate with vegetable oil spray.

In a small bowl, whisk together the lime juice and $1^{1}/_{4}$ teaspoons salt until the salt dissolves. Add the olive oil and adobo sauce and whisk well. Season with pepper, if needed.

When the potatoes are cool enough to handle, remove and discard the skins and slice the potatoes into $^{1}/_{4}$- to $^{1}/_{2}$-inch-thick slices. Brush a little olive oil on the potato slices and season with salt and pepper.

Grill for 2 to 3 minutes on each side. Transfer the grilled potato slices to a serving platter and spoon the vinaigrette on top. Set aside for 10 to 15 minutes to give the potatoes time to absorb the dressing.

Garnish with the scallions and serve.

SERVES 6

vegetable fried rice

Kids love fried rice, as any parent knows who has taken a youngster to a Chinese restaurant. My version employs the lovely Asian flavor infusion of soy, ginger, and garlic and bulks up the rice with plenty of vegetables. This is a good way to use leftover steamed rice and while I make it with white rice, you could just as easily use brown rice.

In a large skillet, heat the oil over medium-high heat until shimmering. Add the garlic and ginger and sauté for 1 minute. Add the carrots, sugar snap peas, scallions, and rice and sauté for 2 to 3 minutes, until the rice is hot.

Add the eggs and peas and cook, stirring continuously, just until the eggs are set. Add the soy sauce and season to taste with salt and pepper. Serve hot.

SERVES 4

1/4 cup canola oil

2 garlic cloves, thinly sliced

2 teaspoons finely grated fresh ginger

1 cup finely diced peeled carrots
   (2 to 3 carrots)

1 cup thinly sliced sugar snap peas
   (3 to 4 ounces)

6 to 7 scallions, trimmed, white and
   green parts thinly sliced

5 cups cold cooked rice

3 large eggs, lightly beaten

1 cup frozen peas

3 tablespoons soy sauce

Salt and freshly ground pepper

Call the Kids
- Peel the carrots with a hand-held peeler
- Measure the rice
- Beat the eggs
- Measure the peas

"hold the anchovies" caesar salad

Caesar salad is an American favorite and kids eagerly join the crowd when it comes to this slightly tangy salad made with crunchy romaine lettuce and crispy croutons. The smooth, creamy dressing plays against the other textures, which makes this salad such a hit. Of course, classic Caesar salad is made with anchovies, but this one does just fine without them. Your kids will probably thank you.

DRESSING

1 to 2 garlic cloves, sliced
2 large egg yolks
Juice of 1 lemon, or more if needed
1 tablespoon Dijon mustard
1 cup extra-virgin olive oil
Salt and freshly ground pepper

SALAD

3 to 4 slices day-old (slightly stale) white bread
3 tablespoons extra-virgin olive oil
Salt and freshly ground pepper
1 head romaine lettuce, washed, dried, and torn into bite-size pieces
$1/2$ cup freshly grated Parmesan cheese, plus extra for serving

Call the Kids

- Squeeze the lemon
- Process the dressing ingredients
- Measure the oil
- Add the olive oil to the dressing
- Wash and dry the lettuce
- Tear the lettuce leaves
- Grate the cheese
- Toss the lettuce with the croutons, cheese, and dressing

To make the dressing, in the bowl of a food processor fitted with the metal blade or in a blender, process the garlic, egg yolks, lemon juice, and mustard for a few seconds. With the motor running, add the oil drop by drop through the feed tube. When about half has been added, continue adding the oil in a slow, steady stream until all is incorporated. If the dressing becomes too thick (it should be the consistency of heavy cream), add a few more drops of lemon juice. When the dressing is emulsified, season with salt and pepper and more lemon juice, if needed. You will have about $1^1/2$ cups of dressing. The dressing can be covered and refrigerated for up to 3 days.

Preheat the oven to 350°F.

Cut the bread into $3/4$-inch cubes and spread out on a rimmed baking sheet. Drizzle with the olive oil and season with salt and pepper. Bake for 10 to 12 minutes, rotating the pan once, until lightly golden brown. Remove from the heat and cool completely.

In a large salad bowl, toss together the lettuce, croutons, and Parmesan. Toss with enough dressing to coat the leaves lightly. Season with salt and pepper, if necessary. Serve immediately topped with extra grated Parmesan cheese.

SERVES 4

grilled corn ratatouille

Corn is not an ingredient ordinarily found in ratatouille, but it tastes good with the eggplant, tomatoes, and squash that form the core of this summertime classic. If the corn is grilled, it adds a faint hint of smokiness, but you could use boiled corn, especially if you have leftovers. It's a side that pairs well with nearly anything, from chicken to steak to fish.

Preheat the oven to 350°F.

Cut the corn kernels from the cobs by standing each ear on its end on a cutting board and slicing the kernels from the lower half of the cob. It is safer to remove only half the kernels at one time and to work from the lower half of the cobs. Turn the cob over and slice off the lower half of the kernels. Reserve the grilled kernels and discard the cobs. Season the corn with salt and pepper.

In a heavy skillet, heat 1 tablespoon of the oil over high heat until shimmering. Add the onion and bell pepper and sauté, stirring occasionally, for about 4 minutes, or until the onion is golden. Add the garlic and cook for 30 to 45 seconds, just until softened but not colored. Transfer to a 2-quart baking dish.

Add another tablespoon of the oil to the skillet, add the zucchini and squash, season with salt and pepper, and sauté for 3 to 4 minutes. Transfer to the dish. Add the eggplant with 2 tablespoons of the oil to the pan, season with salt and pepper, and sauté for 3 to 4 minutes, or until golden. Add the tomatoes and tomato paste and stir to mix. Add the stock, thyme, and bay leaf and cook for a minute or two until well mixed. Transfer to the dish.

Add the remaining tablespoon of oil to the skillet and sauté the grilled corn for 2 to 3 minutes. Add to the dish. Stir in the cayenne.

Cover the baking dish with a lid or foil and bake for 30 minutes, or until heated through and the flavors combine. Taste and adjust the seasoning. Remove the bay leaf and serve warm, at room temperature, or chilled. This can be made ahead and refrigerated for 3 to 4 days.

SERVES 6

3 ears grilled corn (see page 139) or 2 cups boiled corn

Salt and freshly ground pepper

5 tablespoons extra-virgin olive oil

1 small Spanish onion, cut into small dice

1 red bell pepper, seeded and cut into small dice

1 large garlic clove, finely diced

1 medium zucchini, cut into small dice

1 medium yellow squash, cut into small dice

1/2 eggplant, cut into small dice

4 plum tomatoes, seeded and cut into small dice

1 1/2 tablespoons tomato paste

1/3 cup chicken or vegetable stock or low-sodium broth

1 teaspoon chopped fresh thyme leaves

1 bay leaf

Pinch of cayenne pepper

Call the Kids
- Season the raw vegetables
- Mix the vegetables in the casserole
- Pull the thyme leaves off their stems
- Measure the stock
- Add the stock to the skillet

buttermilk onion rings

Whenever I make these, my kids go nuts and I share their enthusiasm. Don't be scared off by the idea of frying. When done correctly, deep-fried food is neither heavy nor greasy. These buttermilk-soaked onion rings are perfectly tender and sweet and taste great alongside burgers and sandwiches, or just as a snack.

3 cups buttermilk

1 cup all-purpose flour, plus more for dredging

1 large white onion

4 cups vegetable oil, for frying (see Note)

Salt and freshly ground pepper

Call the Kids

- Measure then whisk together the buttermilk and flour
- Separate the onion rings
- Put the onion rings in the buttermilk
- Measure the oil
- Lift the rings from the buttermilk
- Dredge the rings in flour
- Salt the fried rings

In a medium shallow bowl, whisk together the buttermilk and flour.

Slice the onion crosswise into substantial slices about $1/2$ inch thick. Carefully separate the slices into rings.

Put the onion rings in the bowl and turn to coat evenly with the buttermilk mixture. Cover the bowl and refrigerate for at least 2 hours and up to 12 hours.

Pour the oil into a heavy, deep pot and heat over medium-high heat until it registers 350°F.

Spread some flour on a plate and season it with salt and pepper. Lift the onion rings from the buttermilk mixture and let any excess drain back into the bowl. Dip the onion rings one at a time in the flour and turn to coat evenly. Fry the onion rings 2 or 3 at a time, turning once, for 2 to 3 minutes, or until lightly golden brown. Lift from the oil with tongs and drain on paper towels. Season with salt and serve immediately.

SERVES 4; MAKES 12 TO 14 ONION RINGS

NOTE: For more tips on deep-frying, see page 61.

bake sales

spiced pumpkin bread ✳ cowboy cookies ✳ white chocolate chip chocolate cookies ✳ cole's confetti cupcakes ✳ chocolate-coconut blondies

You may not be surprised to hear that I am one of the first to sign up for bake sales and holiday celebrations at my kids' schools. A bonus of these activities is how they excite my children. They can't wait to get in the kitchen and start baking with me, and on the day of the bake sale or party, they are bursting with anticipation and end up being proud they helped. I have made each of these recipes for school bake sales and they all are big hits, loved both by the kids and the teachers. The pumpkin bread can be sliced and packed in plastic bags, while the cupcakes stand alone. Carry them to the sale in a bakery box or a large plastic container with a tight-fitting lid. Cowboy Cookies, chock full of raisins and chocolate chips, are perennial favorites and the blondies, flavored with chocolate chips and coconut, are crowd pleasers. Let the kids help pack up the goodies. They can slide slices of bread, cookies, and blondies into plastic bags, or they may want to wrap the cookies or blondies in colorful plastic wrap for a more festive presentation.

spiced pumpkin bread

Scented with cinnamon, cloves, and nutmeg that accent the pumpkin, this bread fills the kitchen with a deliciously impossible-to-resist aroma as it bakes. Canned pumpkin is easy to cook with and so healthful, I like to work it into my kids' meals whenever possible for the vitamin A and C. We slice, wrap, and freeze a loaf or two of this bread for after-school snacks and lunchbox treats; it thaws quickly.

Preheat the oven to 350°F. Spray two 9 x 5 x 3-inch loaf pans with vegetable oil spray.

In a medium bowl, whisk together the flour, baking soda, baking powder, cinnamon, salt, cloves, and nutmeg until evenly mixed. Set aside until needed.

In the bowl of an electric mixer fitted with the paddle attachment and set on medium speed, beat the sugar and butter for 4 to 5 minutes, or until light and fluffy. Add the eggs one at a time. When incorporated, add the pumpkin purée and mix, scraping the bowl occasionally, until smooth.

Reduce the mixer's speed to low and add the orange juice to the batter. Mix until combined. Add the dry ingredients and mix until just combined.

Pour and scrape the batter into the loaf pans, dividing it evenly. Bake for 50 to 55 minutes, or until the centers of the loaves feel dry and firm to the touch and a toothpick inserted in the centers comes out clean.

Invert the loaves and remove from the pans. Let the loaves cool completely right side up on a wire rack.

MAKES TWO 9-INCH LOAVES

Flavorless vegetable oil spray
3 cups all-purpose flour
$1/2$ teaspoon baking soda
2 teaspoons baking powder
2 teaspoons ground cinnamon
$1/2$ teaspoon salt
$1/4$ teaspoon ground cloves
$1/4$ teaspoon ground nutmeg
3 cups sugar
1 cup (2 sticks) unsalted butter, softened
5 large eggs
2 cups canned plain, unseasoned pumpkin purée or one 15-ounce can
$1/4$ cup orange juice

Call the Kids

- Grease the loaf pans with vegetable oil spray
- Measure the flour and sugar
- Measure the pumpkin and juice
- Mix the ingredients together
- Pour the batter into the loaf pans

cowboy cookies

While these are big sellers at bake sales, my kids like to eat them at home, freshly baked and dunked in glasses of cold milk. They are the quintessential oatmeal cookies in that they can be mixed with just about anything you want to make them your personal best cookie-jar treat. I toss in raisins and chocolate chips because I am incapable of making plain oatmeal cookies. I sometimes add coconut or chopped nuts, too.

Flavorless vegetable oil spray

$1^{1}/_{2}$ cups all-purpose flour

1 teaspoon baking soda

$^{1}/_{2}$ teaspoon salt

1 cup (2 sticks) unsalted butter, softened

$^{3}/_{4}$ cup dark brown sugar

$^{3}/_{4}$ cup granulated sugar

2 large eggs

1 teaspoon hot water

1 teaspoon pure vanilla extract

2 cups old-fashioned rolled oats

1 cup raisins or other dried fruit

12 ounces chocolate chips

Preheat the oven to 375°F. Spray 2 baking sheets with the vegetable oil spray.

In a medium bowl, whisk together the flour, baking soda, and salt.

In the bowl of an electric mixer fitted with the paddle attachment, beat the butter and sugars on medium speed for 3 to 4 minutes, until light and fluffy. Stop the mixer to scrape the bowl with a rubber spatula once during this time. Add the eggs one at a time and beat well after each addition. Beat in the water and vanilla.

With the mixer on low speed, add the flour mixture, oats, raisins, and chocolate chips and mix well.

Drop by tablespoonfuls about an inch apart onto the baking sheets. Bake for about 10 minutes, or until lightly golden. Let the cookies rest on the baking sheets for a few minutes before lifting them off with a metal spatula and cooling completely on wire racks. These keep in an airtight container for 4 to 5 days.

MAKES 6 DOZEN COOKIES

Call the Kids

- Grease the baking sheets
- Measure and whisk the flour
- Measure the sugars
- Beat the butter and sugars
- Add the eggs to the batter
- Add the dry ingredients
- Measure the oats
- Mix in the oats, raisins, and chocolate chips
- Drop the cookie dough onto the baking sheets

white chocolate chip chocolate cookies

This crunchy chocolate cookie studded with white chocolate chips is the reverse of most chocolate chip cookies: chocolate dough with white chips (although you could substitute semisweet chocolate chips). Because these are an after-school favorite with my kids, I often freeze half the dough in a plastic container and scoop out spoonfuls of dough to bake whenever we have a hankering for freshly baked cookies. The dough thaws in minutes.

In a medium bowl, whisk together the flour, cocoa, baking soda, and salt. Set aside.

In the bowl of an electric mixer fitted with the paddle attachment and set on medium-high speed, beat together the butter and sugars for 3 to 4 minutes, until light and fluffy. Add the eggs one at a time, mixing well after each addition.

With the mixer on low speed, add the dry ingredients and mix until just blended. Stir in the chocolate chips. Refrigerate the dough for 1 to 2 hours, until firm.

Preheat the oven to 350°F. Grease 2 baking sheets with butter.

Drop rounded teaspoonfuls of the dough 2 inches apart from each other on the baking sheets and bake for 10 to 12 minutes, or until the edges turn crispy.

Let the cookies sit on the baking sheets for a few minutes before lifting them off with a metal spatula and cooling completely on a wire rack. These keep in an airtight container for 4 to 5 days.

MAKES 4 DOZEN COOKIES

1³/₄ cups all-purpose flour

¹/₂ cup unsweetened cocoa powder

1 teaspoon baking soda

¹/₂ teaspoon salt

1 cup (2 sticks) unsalted butter, softened, plus extra for greasing the baking sheets

1 cup packed light brown sugar

¹/₂ cup granulated sugar

2 large eggs

12 ounces white chocolate chips

Call the Kids

- Measure and mix the flour and cocoa
- Measure the sugars
- Beat the butter and sugars
- Add the dry ingredients to the batter
- Stir in the chocolate chips
- Grease the baking sheets
- Drop the cookie dough onto the baking sheets

cole's confetti cupcakes

My son Cole loves vanilla above all other flavors (even chocolate), so these are for him. I make them with cake flour because it results in a very light, moist, soft-crumbed cupcake. Everyone likes the frosting, which is pretty hard to resist. I lick the bowl more than once when I make it! This is the same recipe we use for the cupcakes we sell at our stores, and we sell a lot of them—for our adult customers and their kids.

2 cups cake flour

$2^1/_2$ teaspoons baking powder

Pinch of salt

1 cup sugar

$^1/_2$ cup (1 stick) unsalted butter,
    softened

4 large egg yolks

$^2/_3$ cup milk

1 teaspoon pure vanilla extract

Vanilla Frosting (recipe follows)

Decorative sprinkles, such as confetti,
    rainbow, or others

Call the Kids

- Put the paper liners into the pan
- Measure the flour
- Whisk together the flour, baking powder, and salt
- Measure the sugar
- Beat the sugar and butter
- Mix together the yolks, milk, and vanilla
- Mix the batter
- Fill the cupcake liners
- Measure and mix the frosting ingredients
- Frost the cupcakes

Preheat the oven to 350°F. Insert paper cupcake liners into a 12-cup muffin pan.

Put the flour, baking powder, and salt in a small bowl, whisk well, and set aside.

In the bowl of an electric mixer fitted with the paddle attachment, beat together the sugar and butter on medium speed for 5 to 6 minutes, or until light and fluffy.

Reduce the speed to low and slowly add the dry ingredients until the mixture is crumbly like cornmeal.

Meanwhile, in a small bowl, combine the yolks, milk, and vanilla extract. Slowly add to the batter, scraping the bottom of the bowl once or twice.

Spoon the batter into the paper cupcake liners, filling each about three-quarters full. Bake for about 18 minutes, or until light golden brown.

Remove from the oven and allow to cool on wire racks in the pan.

When the cupcakes are cool, frost with vanilla frosting, and then decorate as desired.

MAKES 12 CUPCAKES

vanilla frosting

In the bowl of an electric mixer fitted with the paddle attachment, beat the butter, sugar, milk, and vanilla extract together on medium speed until well combined and creamy.

MAKES ABOUT 2$^1/_2$ CUPS

$^1/_2$ cup (1 stick) unsalted butter, softened
1 pound confectioners' sugar (about 4 cups)
3 tablespoons milk
1 teaspoon pure vanilla extract

chocolate-coconut blondies

Chocolate and coconut is a great flavor combination, as anyone who likes Mounds bars can attest! I bring them together in these deliciously moist blondies. Blondies have gotten a bad rap because some can be on the dry side, but these put those claims to rest, once and for all. I promise, these will get the same raves as the chocolate Turtle Brownies on page 71.

Preheat the oven to 350°F. Spray an 8-inch square baking pan with vegetable oil spray.

In a medium bowl, whisk together the flour and baking powder and set aside.

In the bowl of an electric mixer with the paddle attachment, beat the butter and the brown sugar at medium-high speed for 3 to 5 minutes, until light and fluffy, stopping the mixer to scrape the bowl occasionally. Add the eggs one at a time, beating after each one to incorporate. Add the vanilla extract.

With the mixer on low speed, add the dry ingredients and mix until mostly incorporated. Add the water and mix until combined. Add the chocolate chips and coconut and beat until well mixed.

Spoon the batter into the baking pan and smooth the surface. Bake for 25 to 30 minutes, or until set and a toothpick inserted in the center comes out dry. Set the pan on a wire cooling rack. When completely cool, cut into squares.

MAKES 12 TO 16 BLONDIES

Flavorless vegetable oil spray
1$^3/_4$ cups all-purpose flour
1 teaspoon baking powder
$^3/_4$ cup (1$^1/_2$ sticks) unsalted butter, softened
1$^1/_2$ cups packed light brown sugar
2 large eggs
1$^1/_2$ teaspoons vanilla extract
$^1/_4$ cup water
1$^1/_2$ cups semisweet chocolate chips
1 cup sweetened coconut flakes

Call the Kids

- Grease the pan
- Measure the sugar
- Measure the flour
- Measure the water
- Measure the chocolate chips and coconut

desserts

summer pound cake ✳ remy's patchwork apple pie ✳ ginger shortcakes with nectarines and blueberries ✳ deep dark gingerbread with crystallized ginger whipped cream ✳ creamy chocolate-cinnamon pudding with whipped cream ✳ rhubarb, strawberry, and apple crisp ✳ french toast bread pudding ✳ marble swirl cheesecake ✳ great aunt lottie's homestyle chocolate cake ✳ warm molten chocolate cakes

When I began cooking as a kid, I was always most enthusiastic about dessert and couldn't wait to get started once I found a tempting recipe. And then I couldn't wait to finish the first part of the meal and sample the result! Most kids begin with simple desserts when they learn to cook. They want to help because they know they genuinely like dessert and eagerly look forward to the end result. And, above all, the process is fun, from licking the bowl to tasting the finished product, which makes gratification possible every step of the way. I include recipes that cover a wide range of tastes and techniques, from cookies and shortcakes to fruit desserts and an absolutely irresistible chocolate cake.

summer pound cake

Although this is a perfect moist summer cake with delicate lemon flavor, it's equally good any time of year. You can slice it and have it as an afternoon snack or serve it with a glass of iced tea. You can also doll it up with fresh berries and whipped cream or ice cream for a full-blown dessert.

Preheat the oven to 350°F. Lightly butter a 10-inch tube pan or Bundt pan. Make sure the tube is well greased as well as the sides and bottom of the pan.

Put the flour, baking powder, and salt in a small bowl, whisk well, and set aside.

In the bowl of an electric mixer fitted with the paddle attachment, beat the butter at medium speed until smooth. Slowly add the sugar, scraping the sides of the bowl once or twice, and beat for 4 to 5 minutes, or until light and fluffy.

Add the eggs a little at a time, beating after each addition and continuing to beat until fully incorporated and the mixture is light and fluffy.

Reduce the speed to low and add the flour mixture alternately with the milk, beginning and ending with the dry ingredients. Slowly beat in the zest, juice, and vanilla.

Pour the batter into the prepared pan and bake for 45 to 50 minutes, or until the cake springs back when gently pressed and a toothpick inserted near its center comes out clean.

Cool the cake in the pan for 10 minutes. Invert the cake over a wire rack and lift the pan off the cake. If the cake sticks, run a dull kitchen knife around the cake. Cool right side up on a wire rack. Wrapped well in plastic wrap, this can keep for 2 to 3 days.

MAKES ONE 10-INCH TUBE CAKE

1 cup (2 sticks) unsalted butter, softened, plus extra for greasing the tube pan
3 cups all-purpose flour
2 teaspoons baking powder
1/2 teaspoon salt
2 cups sugar
3 large eggs, lightly beaten
1 cup milk
Grated zest of 2 lemons
Juice of 1 lemon
2 teaspoons pure vanilla extract

Call the Kids

- Grease the pan
- Measure the flour
- Whisk the dry ingredients
- Measure the sugar
- Beat the eggs lightly
- Measure the milk
- Add the eggs, dry ingredients, and milk to the batter
- Squeeze the lemon and add the juice to the batter
- Pour the batter into the pan
- Prepare the whipped cream or berries or both, for serving

remy's patchwork apple pie

My daughter Remy loves apples and so I am not surprised she loves this pie and always helps me make it. It's a foolproof pie for kids because it only has one crust—on top—and the dough doesn't even need to be rolled. Little hands can flatten it before cutting it into squares to place over the filling in a patchwork pattern. And perhaps most important, the sweet, reassuring apple flavor is out of this world.

7 Golden Delicious, Granny Smith,
   or Fuji apples

$1/2$ cup raisins

$3/4$ cup plus 1 tablespoon sugar

$1/2$ cup (1 stick) unsalted butter,
   softened

1 large egg

$1^{1}/2$ cups all-purpose flour, plus more
   for sprinkling

1 tablespoon heavy cream

1 teaspoon ground cinnamon

$1/4$ cup finely chopped walnuts
   (optional)

Call the Kids

- Core the apples with a hand-held corer
- Lay the apples in the pie plate
- Measure and scatter the raisins over the apples
- Measure the sugar and flour for the dough
- Mix the dough
- Flatten the dough into a crust
- Lay the crust squares over the apples
- Measure and stir together the cinnamon topping
- Sprinkle the topping over the crust

Preheat the oven to 375°F.

Peel, core, and slice the apples into $1/4$-inch slices. Cover the bottom of a 9-inch deep-dish pie plate with the apple slices and sprinkle with the raisins.

In the bowl of an electric mixer fitted with the paddle attachment, beat $3/4$ cup of the sugar and the butter on medium speed for 4 to 5 minutes, or until light and fluffy. Add the egg and then the $1^{1}/2$ cups flour and mix well.

Sprinkle a work surface with about $1/4$ cup flour. Turn the dough out onto the work surface and work it by hand as you flatten it into a crust that is $1/4$ to $1/2$ inch thick. (You could also roll the dough with a rolling pin.) Pat the dough lightly to flatten it. Cut the crust into 2-inch squares and lay these over the apples to create a patchwork effect. Brush with the cream.

In a small bowl, stir together the remaining tablespoon of sugar, the cinnamon, and the walnuts, if using. Sprinkle over the crust and bake for 15 minutes. Lower the oven temperature to 350°F. and bake for 30 to 35 minutes longer, or until the crust is golden brown and the apples are bubbly. Serve warm or at room temperature.

MAKES ONE 9-INCH PIE

rhubarb, strawberry apple crisp moved to page to make room for photos.

ginger shortcakes with nectarines and blueberries

Shortcakes may be nothing more than an excuse to eat piles of fruit topped with whipped cream, but the flaky biscuit bases for these are speckled with ginger, which makes them truly special. In fact, I frequently bake them in the winter to serve as ginger scones. For this summer dessert, I suggest nectarines and blueberries, although you can use any other fruit that is ripe and plentiful.

Preheat the oven to 350°F.

In the bowl of an electric mixer fitted with the paddle attachment, mix together the flour, granulated sugar, baking powder, baking soda, ginger, and salt. With the mixer on low, add the butter and mix until the mixture is the consistency of cornmeal.

Add the buttermilk and crystallized ginger and mix on low just until the dough comes together.

Turn the dough out onto a lightly floured work surface and flatten with your hands or a rolling pin until the dough is 1/4 to 1/2 inch thick. Using a 3-inch round biscuit or cookie cutter, or a drinking glass, stamp out 4 to 5 circles. Reroll the dough to cut 1 to 2 more shortcakes. You should have 6 rounds.

Put the shortcake rounds on an ungreased baking sheet. Brush the tops with 2 tablespoons of the heavy cream and bake for 20 to 25 minutes, or until light golden brown.

Meanwhile, in the chilled bowl of an electric mixer fitted with the whisk attachment, whip the remaining cup of heavy cream on high speed with the confectioners' sugar until it holds stiff peaks, 5 to 6 minutes. Reserve.

Cut each nectarine in half and remove the pit. Slice each half into 6 pieces. You will have 24 slices. Rinse and dry the blueberries.

Slice each shortcake in half and dollop whipped cream on each of the bottom halves. Top with nectarine slices and blueberries. Replace the tops and serve.

MAKES 6 SHORTCAKES

1 1/2 cups all-purpose flour

2 1/2 tablespoons granulated sugar

2 1/2 teaspoons baking powder

1/2 teaspoon baking soda

1 1/2 teaspoons ground ginger

1/2 teaspoon salt

6 tablespoons cold unsalted butter, cubed

1/2 cup buttermilk

3/4 cup chopped crystallized ginger

1 cup plus 2 tablespoons heavy cream

1 tablespoon confectioners' sugar

2 ripe nectarines

1/2 pint blueberries

Call the Kids

- Measure the flour
- Mix the flour, sugar, baking powder, baking soda, ground ginger, and salt
- Cut up the butter with a blunt knife
- Measure the buttermilk
- Measure the ginger
- Measure the cream
- Mix the dough
- Pat the dough flat
- Stamp out shortcakes
- Brush the shortcakes with cream
- Wash the blueberries
- Whip the cream
- Assemble the shortcakes

deep dark gingerbread with crystallized ginger whipped cream

Gingerbread is one of the more rewarding things to make. It smells so good while it bakes and then, when it's done, it can be paired with any number of delicious things, from cinnamon ice cream to lemon curd. Or, do as I suggest here and serve it with this fabulous whipped cream.

GINGERBREAD

1 tablespoon melted butter

3 1/2 cups all-purpose flour, plus extra for the pan

1 tablespoon plus 2 teaspoons ground ginger

2 teaspoons baking soda

1/2 teaspoon ground cloves

1/2 teaspoon salt

1 cup (2 sticks) unsalted butter, softened

1 1/2 cups packed dark brown sugar

2 large eggs

2 cups molasses

1 cup boiling water

CRYSTALLIZED GINGER WHIPPED CREAM

1 1/2 cups heavy cream

1 tablespoon confectioners' sugar

1/2 cup finely chopped crystallized ginger

Call the Kids

- Butter and flour the pan
- Measure the flour
- Whisk together the flour, ginger, baking soda, cloves, and salt
- Beat the butter and sugar
- Measure the molasses
- Add the eggs and molasses to the batter
- Add the dry ingredients to the batter
- Measure and whip the cream

Preheat the oven to 350°F. Brush a 10-inch tube pan with the melted butter and dust with flour. Tap out the excess flour. Make sure the tube is well greased and floured as well as the sides and bottom of the pan.

In a medium bowl, whisk together the flour, ground ginger, baking soda, cloves, and salt. Set aside.

In the bowl of an electric mixer fitted with a paddle attachment and set on medium-high speed, beat the butter and sugar until light and fluffy, 3 to 5 minutes. Add the eggs one at a time, beating after each addition. Slowly add the molasses and mix until well blended.

With the mixer on medium-low speed, gradually add the dry ingredients to the batter just until combined.

Remove the bowl from the mixer and using a rubber spatula, stir in the boiling water, 1/2 cup at a time.

Pour the batter into the tube pan and bake for about 50 minutes, or until the cake just feels firm and begins to pull away from the sides of the pan.

Cool the cake in the pan on a wire rack for about 30 minutes. Invert the pan and remove the cake. If necessary, run a dull kitchen knife around the cake and around the tube to loosen it.

Meanwhile, in a chilled bowl of an electric mixer fitted with the whisk attachment, whip the cream and confectioners' sugar on medium-high speed. When the cream begins to thicken, add the crystallized ginger. Continue to beat on medium-high speed until the cream forms stiff peaks.

Serve the cake warm or at room temperature, with the whipped cream.

SERVES 12 TO 14

creamy chocolate-cinnamon pudding with whipped cream

There's not a kid alive who doesn't love rich, creamy chocolate pudding. I enhance it with cinnamon to invoke the flavors of Mexican hot chocolate. The better the cocoa and chocolate you can find, the better the pudding. You can make a big bowl of this or pour it into individual ramekins.

In the top of a double boiler over barely simmering water, melt the chocolate and butter. Stir to combine and remove from the heat. Alternatively, put the chocolate and butter in a glass measuring cup or similar container and microwave on medium-high power for 50 to 60 seconds. When the butter melts and the chocolate softens so that it looks shiny, stir until smooth.

In a medium bowl, whisk together the cocoa, $1/3$ cup of the sugar, the cornstarch, and cinnamon. Whisk in $1/2$ cup of the milk until blended. Whisk in the egg and egg yolks.

In a saucepan, combine the remaining cup of milk, the remaining $1/4$ cup of sugar, and the heavy cream and bring to a gentle simmer over medium-low heat. Slowly whisk about $1/2$ cup of the hot milk mixture into the cocoa mixture to temper it.

Return this to the saucepan and, whisking constantly, bring to a gentle boil. Cook, still whisking, for 30 seconds.

Remove from the heat and immediately pour into six 8-ounce custard cups or ramekins. Cover each with plastic wrap so that the plastic rests directly on the custard to prevent a skin from forming. Cool for 1 hour at room temperature, and then refrigerate until thoroughly chilled, at least 2 hours or for up to 12 hours.

Serve the puddings topped with dollops of whipped cream.

SERVES 6

4 ounces semisweet or bittersweet chocolate, chopped
2 tablespoons unsalted butter
$1/4$ cup unsweetened cocoa powder
$1/3$ cup plus $1/4$ cup sugar
2 tablespoons cornstarch
$1/2$ teaspoon ground cinnamon
$1 1/2$ cups milk
1 large egg
2 large egg yolks
$1/2$ cup heavy cream
Sweetened Whipped Cream (recipe follows)

Call the Kids

- Measure the cocoa and sugar
- Measure the milk
- Whisk in the milk and eggs
- Cover the ramekins with plastic wrap
- Measure and whip the cream
- Dollop the cream on the puddings

sweetened whipped cream

In the chilled bowl of an electric mixer fitted with the whisk attachment and set on medium-high speed, beat the cream, sugar, and vanilla until the cream forms stiff peaks. Alternatively, whisk the cream by hand with a large wire whisk.

MAKES ABOUT 2 CUPS

1 cup heavy cream
1 tablespoon plus 1 teaspoon confectioners' sugar
1 teaspoon vanilla extract

rhubarb, strawberry, and apple crisp

As much as I like to eat fresh fruit, there is something about the texture and flavor of baked fruit that I find irresistible. And nowhere is this more apparent than in a crisp, where the crunchy, sweet crumb topping plays off the fruit wonderfully. Make this with rhubarb and strawberries in the spring or with pears in the fall. I bake crisps right before dinner so that they are still warm when it's time for dessert.

4 large Fuji, Granny Smith, or Golden Delicious apples, peeled, cored, and cut into 1-inch chunks (about 4 cups)

3 large rhubarb stalks, cut into 1-inch pieces (about 2 cups)

1 pint strawberries, hulled and cut into quarters (about 2 cups)

1/4 cup all-purpose flour

1 cup sugar

TOPPING

6 tablespoons unsalted butter, softened

1/4 cup granulated sugar

1/4 cup packed dark brown sugar

3/4 teaspoon ground cinnamon

Pinch of salt

3 cups all-purpose flour

1/2 cup old-fashioned rolled oats

Sweetened Whipped Cream (page 181) or ice cream (optional)

Preheat the oven to 350°F.

Combine the apples, rhubarb, and strawberries in a large bowl and toss with the flour and sugar until the fruit begins releasing its juice. This will take 2 to 3 minutes.

To make the topping, in the bowl of an electric mixer fitted with the paddle attachment combine the butter, sugars, cinnamon, salt, and flour and mix on medium speed until crumbly. Stir in the oats by hand. You can refrigerate the topping in a lidded container for up to 1 month.

Distribute the fruit evenly in a 9 x 11-inch baking pan. Sprinkle the crumb topping over the fruit and bake for 35 to 40 minutes, or until the topping is golden and the fruit is bubbling.

Serve warm or at room temperature with whipped cream or ice cream, if desired.

SERVES 8 TO 10

Call the Kids
- Peel the apples with a hand-held peeler
- Hull and cut the strawberries with a blunt knife
- Measure the flour and sugar
- Toss the fruit with the flour and sugar
- Measure the sugar, flour, and oats for the crumb topping
- Mix the crumb topping
- Sprinkle the topping over the fruit

french toast bread pudding

If you are a French toast lover, as I am, you will love this dessert. And if you are wild about bread pudding, even better. Because I always embellish French toast with vanilla and cinnamon, it was a natural transition to turn this into a dessert. Nothing fancy or tricky here—just pure comfort food.

Preheat the oven to 325°F. Grease a 13 x 9 x 2-inch baking dish with butter.

In a large bowl, combine the milk, cream, eggs, egg yolks, brown sugar, $^1/_2$ cup of the granulated sugar, the vanilla, 1 teaspoon of the cinnamon, and the nutmeg. Mix well.

Add the bread cubes to the bowl and stir gently. Set aside to soak for 10 to 15 minutes.

Gently stir in the raisins and pour the mixture into the baking dish.

In a small bowl, stir together the remaining 2 tablespoons of granulated sugar and 1 teaspoon of cinnamon. Sprinkle over the bread pudding. Bake for about 40 minutes, or until just set. Serve warm or at room temperature.

SERVES 8 TO 10

Unsalted butter

2 cups milk

2 cups heavy cream

3 large eggs

2 large egg yolks

$^1/_2$ cup packed light brown sugar

$^1/_2$ cup plus 2 tablespoons granulated sugar

1 teaspoon pure vanilla extract

2 teaspoons ground cinnamon

$^1/_2$ teaspoon freshly grated nutmeg

8 cups cubed white bread or brioche (10 to 11 slices)

$^3/_4$ cup raisins

Call the Kids
- Grease the pan
- Measure the milk, cream, and sugars
- Mix the milk, cream, eggs, sugars, vanilla, and spices
- Pour the milk mixture over the bread cubes
- Measure the raisins
- Mix the sugar and cinnamon
- Sprinkle the topping over the pudding

marble swirl cheesecake

When I made this recipe as a kid, I remember being fascinated by how the two batters swirled together and how no two cheesecakes ever looked exactly alike. The rich chocolate flavors complement the sweetness of the vanilla batter, making a perfect dessert for special occasions.

Unsalted butter

1½ cups graham cracker crumbs
(10 or 11 whole crackers)

3 tablespoons melted unsalted butter

2 pounds cream cheese, softened

1⅓ cups sugar

4 large eggs

2 teaspoons pure vanilla extract

2 cups (1 pint) heavy cream

7 ounces semisweet or bittersweet chocolate, coarsely chopped

⅓ cup water

Call the Kids

- Grease the pan
- Put the graham crackers in a plastic bag and roll over them with a rolling pin until crushed
- Mix the graham cracker crust
- Press the crust into the pan
- Measure the sugar
- Beat the cream cheese and sugar
- Measure the cream
- Add the eggs, vanilla, and cream
- Measure the water
- Marble the chocolate batter with the vanilla batter

Preheat the oven to 325°F. Grease a 9-inch cake pan that is 3 to 4 inches deep with butter.

In a medium bowl, combine the graham cracker crumbs and melted butter and mix well. Press the mixture evenly into the bottom of the cake pan. Bake for about 10 minutes, or until the crust is just set and slightly firm. Remove from the oven and set aside on a wire rack to cool. Lower the oven temperature to 300°F.

In the bowl of an electric mixer fitted with the paddle attachment and set on medium-high speed, beat the cream cheese and sugar together until smooth, 3 to 4 minutes, scraping down the sides of the bowl once or twice.

Add the eggs one at a time, and beat after each addition until smooth. Add the vanilla and cream, beat well, and scrape the sides of the bowl once or twice. Remove 1 cup of the batter and set aside while you melt the chocolate.

In the top of a double boiler over barely simmering water, combine the chocolate and water and let the chocolate melt. Remove the top of the double boiler or bowl from the heat and stir until smooth. Mix the reserved cup of vanilla batter into the melted chocolate.

Pour the vanilla batter from the mixing bowl into the prepared pan. Pour or spoon the chocolate batter over the top of the vanilla batter in a circle. Run a small knife through the chocolate and vanilla batters to create a marbleized effect. Don't overdo it or the two will simply mix together.

Put the cheesecake in a larger pan such as a roasting pan. Add enough hot water to the larger pan to come halfway up the sides of the cake pan. Bake for 1 hour and 45 minutes. Turn off the oven and let the cheesecake sit in the oven for another hour.

Remove the cake from the oven and set aside on a wire rack until cooled to room temperature. Cover and refrigerate overnight or for at least 8 hours. Serve chilled.

SERVES 10 TO 12

great aunt lottie's homestyle chocolate cake

This is an incredible chocolate cake that our customers at Aux Délices—not to mention my kids—can't get enough of. Something about the combination of the cake and the chocolate cream cheese frosting makes it absolutely memorable. It's the kind of old-fashioned chocolate cake that never goes out of style.

Preheat the oven to 350°F. Spray two 8-inch cake pans with vegetable oil spray. Cut out 2 parchment paper rounds to fit in the bottom of each pan and insert them in the pans. Spray the paper lightly with vegetable oil spray.

In the bowl of an electric mixer fitted with the paddle attachment, stir together the flour, sugar, cocoa, baking powder, and salt. Add the shortening and butter and with the mixer on low speed, mix until the batter has the consistency of cornmeal.

In a large glass measuring cup or small mixing bowl, stir the baking soda into the coffee. This will foam. Increase the mixer's speed to medium and add the coffee to the batter. Add the eggs and the vanilla and mix well.

Divide the batter evenly between the cake pans and smooth the surfaces with a rubber spatula. Bake for about 25 minutes, or until a toothpick inserted in the center of a cake layer comes out dry. Cool in the pans for about 10 minutes before inverting the cakes onto wire racks to cool completely.

When the cake layers are completely cool, put one on a platter or cardboard round and spread about a third of the frosting over the bottom layer. (You may want to level the top of the bottom layer first by slicing the domed portion of the cake off with a serrated knife.) Put the top layer on the cake and frost the sides and top of the cake with the remaining frosting.

SERVES 10 TO 12

Flavorless vegetable oil spray

2^1/$_4$ cups sifted all-purpose flour

1^1/$_2$ cups sugar

4^1/$_2$ tablespoons unsweetened cocoa powder

1^1/$_2$ teaspoons baking powder

^{1}/$_4$ teaspoon salt

^{1}/$_4$ cup solid vegetable shortening, such as Crisco

4 tablespoons (^{1}/$_2$ stick) unsalted butter, softened

1^1/$_2$ teaspoons baking soda

1^1/$_2$ cups strong, hot brewed coffee

2 large eggs, slightly beaten

1^1/$_2$ teaspoons pure vanilla extract

Homestyle Chocolate Frosting (page 187)

Call the Kids
- Spray the pans with vegetable oil spray
- Trace and cut out the parchment paper rounds
- Measure the flour
- Sift the flour, baking soda, baking powder, and salt
- Measure the sugar and cocoa powder
- Mix the batter
- Measure the vegetable shortening
- Add the eggs to the batter
- Fill the cake pans
- Measure and mix the frosting
- Frost the cake

homestyle chocolate frosting

In a medium bowl, whisk together the cocoa and confectioners' sugar until blended and the color is nearly uniform.

In the bowl of an electric mixer fitted with the paddle attachment, beat the cream cheese on medium speed until slightly softened. Reduce the speed to low and add the cocoa mixture. Beat until well combined.

Add the milk and vanilla extract and beat for 2 to 3 minutes, or until smooth, scraping the bowl once or twice during the mixing process.

NOTE: The frosting freezes very well. Scrape it into a plastic freezer bag or lidded plastic container. It freezes for up to 2 months and defrosts in a few hours at room temperature.

MAKES ABOUT 3 CUPS

1 cup plus 1 tablespoon unsweetened cocoa powder

1 pound confectioners' sugar (about 4 cups)

9 ounces cream cheese, softened

3 tablespoons milk

1 teaspoon pure vanilla extract

warm molten chocolate cakes

Warm chocolate cakes with soft, liquid centers are still popular in restaurants, and yet are easy to make at home, whether you're making them to impress dinner guests or your family. Who doesn't love a warm dessert? It's the height of luxury! Best of all, you can make these ahead of time, refrigerate or freeze them, and pop them in the oven minutes before serving.

5 tablespoons unsalted butter, softened, plus more for buttering the molds

5 ounces bittersweet or semisweet chocolate, coarsely chopped

4 large eggs

Scant $1/4$ cup sugar

$1/4$ cup plus $1 1/2$ teaspoons sifted cake flour

6 Chocolate Ganache Balls (recipe follows)

Sweetened Whipped Cream (page 181) or ice cream (optional)

Call the Kids
- Butter the molds
- Measure the sugar
- Mix the batter
- Measure and add the flour
- Put the ganache balls in molds filled with batter

Preheat the oven to 400°F. Generously butter six 4-ounce molds or ramekins.

In the top of a double boiler over barely simmering water, melt the butter and chocolate. Stir to combine and remove from the heat. Alternatively, put the chocolate and butter in a glass measuring cup or similar container and microwave on medium-high power for 50 to 60 seconds. When the butter melts and the chocolate softens so that it looks shiny, stir until smooth. Microwave for another 30 or 40 seconds, if necessary.

In the bowl of an electric mixer fitted with the whisk attachment, beat the eggs and sugar together on high speed until the mixture increases in volume and is pale yellow in color, about 5 minutes.

Reduce the speed of the mixer to low and add the flour. Pour in the melted chocolate and butter mixture and mix well.

Fill the buttered molds halfway with the batter. Put a ganache ball in the center of each mold and then fill them with batter so that they are three-quarters full and the ganache is covered. Refrigerate for at least 30 minutes or up to 2 to 3 days or freeze until ready to use.

Bake the cakes for 12 minutes or until the tops are set, look dry, and your finger leaves a mark in the top of a cake mold when gently pressed. (If cakes have been frozen, bake for 14 minutes.)

Allow the cakes to rest in their molds for 1 minute. Run a small, dull knife around the edge of each mold and unmold onto serving plates. Serve with whipped cream or ice cream, if desired.

MAKES 6 SERVINGS

chocolate ganache balls

Put the chocolate in a mixing bowl.

In a small saucepan, heat the cream over medium heat until it begins to form a skin on the surface. Pour the hot cream over the chocolate and whisk until smooth.

Let the chocolate ganache cool to room temperature. It will thicken as it does. Cover and refrigerate until solid.

Using a teaspoon, break off small balls of ganache. With dampened palms, roll the ganache into as many small balls as needed. Set the balls aside on a wax paper–lined plate or tray until needed. Refrigerate the balls if they will sit at room temperature for more than a few minutes.

NOTE: The recipe makes more than you need, so freeze the extra balls in a zippered plastic bag or container to have on hand for the next time you make Warm Molten Chocolate Cakes. You can also pop them in hot chocolate or melt them down for an ice cream topping. You could even coat them with cocoa or confectioners' sugar for easy chocolate truffles.

MAKES A GENEROUS ³/₄ CUP; MORE THAN ENOUGH FOR 18 BALLS

4 ounces bittersweet or semisweet
   chocolate, cut up into small pieces
¹/₂ cup heavy cream

index